think
like
a
SheEO

SUCCEEDING IN THE
AGE OF CREATORS, MAKERS,
AND ENTREPRENEURS

Vicki Saunders *with M.J. Ryan*

Copyright © Vicki Saunders, 2014

ISBN 978-1502103658

Orders:

SheEO Press
375 Markham St.
Toronto, Ontario M6G 2K8
Canada

Cover Design: Lisa Marie Bettencourt

For more information, visit www.iamasheeo.com

Twitter: @iamasheeo
FB: https://222.facebook.com/sheeoofficial

SheEO Press
375 Markham St.
Toronto, Ontario, M6G 2K8
Canada

To Richard, for your limitless thinking, endless capacity
for deep listening, and your pure joy for life

To A&B, for always being there, no matter what

To Aidan, Molly, Keegan, Jade, Brendan, Julia, Finn,
and Sienna, for giving me the space to be goofy,
wise, and playful

CONTENTS

Until one is committed, there is hesitancy, the chance to draw back. Concerning all acts of initiative (and creation), there is one elementary truth, the ignorance of which kills countless ideas and splendid plans: that the moment one definitely commits oneself, then Providence moves too. All sorts of things occur to help one that would never otherwise have occurred. A whole stream of events issues from the decision, raising in one's favor all manner of unforeseen incidents and meetings and material assistance, which no man could have dreamed would have come his way. Whatever you can do, or dream you can do, begin it. Boldness has genius, power, and magic in it. Begin it now.

—Johann Wolfgang von Goethe

Members of the first SheEO cohort gather to celebrate the end of the program that builds new networks and confidence to lead on your own terms.

Bottom row (left to right): Cathy Han, Tash Jeffries, Bianca Sayan, Sarah Grossman, Sherene Ng.

Top row (left to right): Lauren Long, Jessica Knox, Julie Forand, Anne Pringle, Jane Wu, Consuelo McAlister.

INTRODUCTION
THE BIRTH OF A NEW MINDSET

You never change things by fighting the existing reality. To change something, build a new model that makes the existing model obsolete.

—Buckminster Fuller

We are at a moment in history that is simply breathtaking. A quick look out the window and it's clear that we need to redefine, redesign, and recreate almost every aspect of society. Large corporations, small companies, political leaders, entertainers—pretty much everyone you talk to realizes that what we're doing isn't working. The game we created is on its last legs. Jobs are disappearing and not likely to come back. One percent of the population holds the majority of the wealth. Our systems are bursting at the seams, operating at an unsustainable pace. We need new thinking, new approaches, new ways of being and working that work for all of humanity. We need SheEOs.

SheEOs are women who leverage their passions and strengths to create businesses that build new models, new mindsets, and new solutions for a better world. SheEOs discover their own path and create success on their own terms. They experiment to find what matters to them, listen to what motivates them, notice when they're in the zone and when they aren't, and tweak things to maximize their energy for impact. They step back to look at what's working and what's not, iterating and experimenting, partnering with others for increased success and impact.

SheEOs are at the forefront of what I call the age of creators, makers, and entrepreneurs. We've all heard the term *entrepreneur*. According to a 2013 Pollara study published in *The Globe and Mail*, almost half of Canadian post-secondary students want to be entrepreneurs, a huge upswing in the numbers over the past decades. At the same time, the maker movement is well underway, a movement that's all about creating and sharing ideas and spreading designs. Some say that it's basically a scrappy do-it-yourself (DIY) and do it-with-others (DIWO) movement that encompasses engineering, electronics, robotics, 3D printing, arts and crafts, woodworking, and jewelry-making. Jeremy Rifkin would say that it's the power-to-the-people start of the third industrial revolution on the way to what he calls the shareable economy.

We used to talk about small- and medium-sized enterprises (SMEs) as being the engine of the economy. But in the distributed, networked, peer-to-peer collaborative world we're entering, it's the CMEs—creators, makers, and entrepreneurs—who are the fuel that will get us to a better future. And SheEOs are leading the way with their energy, creativity, and unwillingness to do business as usual.

MY SheEO JOURNEY

I remember the moment I became a SheEO, although I didn't have the word for it at the time. It had nothing to do with starting a business, at least not at first. It was a shift in mindset, a change in mental model of the world and my place in it. It was 1989. I was in Europe taking some time away to decide whether to do a PhD. One morning I sat down at the table, picked up the *International Herald Tribune*, and saw that the Berlin Wall had fallen. (For those of you too young to remember a wall in Eastern Europe, there used to be one. It was a big deal—Google it.) I looked at my brother, whom I was staying with at the time, and said, "Let's go!"

There was so much energy in Prague, the capital of what is now the Czech Republic. Hundreds of thousands of people lined the streets to be together and to hear the well-known dissident Vaclav Havel address the newly freed nation. Every single conversation I heard in Prague started with the phrase *Now that I'm free*: "Now that I'm free I'm going to start a business." "Now that I'm free I'm going to quit my job." "Now that I'm free I'm going to travel."

After a couple of weeks sitting in pubs and cafés, overhearing this excitement and these dreams of the future, it suddenly dawned on me: "I'm free, too. What am I going to do?" I was born in Canada, one of the most amazing free countries in the world, but for some reason I'd never really felt free. There were restrictions on what was possible, or so I thought. It wasn't until that moment in Prague that I realized deep down that I could do anything with my life.

In hindsight, the most incredible part of that experience—one that has affected me ever since—was the privilege of witnessing an entire nation flip a switch in their brains and change how they thought. One day there are tanks in your country, and the next day they're gone and suddenly everyone is liberated.

Prague opened up my eyes to a whole new world of possibilities. I guess I'd always somehow known that I could do anything I wanted. Or at least I should have known. My parents were very supportive and told me I could do anything, but society's norms seeped in over time. There are certain jobs that are respected, schools that have prestige, salaries that are worthy. Over time, I picked up a lot of cultural cues that influenced who I was. And most of those cues were external, driving me in a direction that was acceptable to my peers, my family, my teachers, my community. There were unwritten rules about being safe and getting a job, or following the money, or doing charity work. But I always felt I was between the cracks of the traditional paths people took. I wanted to make money and yet I wanted to do good. I wanted to work hard and yet I wanted to be free to travel. Back then, such ideas were considered unrealistic: "Oh, Vicki, just go get a job. You're smart. You can do anything. Make a lot of money and then do your 'social' stuff."

Prague blew the top off the pot and helped me get outside the box I'd created for myself. In one fell swoop it was as though everything that had been limiting me fell away and I had a chance to be a whole new person.

I remember an *Oprah* show where she said something like, "You know when you hear a little *psst*, and you look around thinking, 'Did I hear something? Nope, okay, I'll just keep doing what I'm doing.' Then you get a little flick on the ear and wonder, 'What was that? Hmm, must not be anything.' And you keep doing what you're doing. Then you get a whack on the side of the head and think, 'What the heck?' And you still keep doing what you're doing. Then a house falls on you and you finally get the message." Well, that was Prague for me. I'd had all the right instincts since I was very young. We all do. We know what's right for us. And yet even though we know what works and what doesn't, we often discount that knowledge and think we're the ones who are wrong. We trust the external voices rather than our internal ones—until we have an experience as I did in Prague, or as others do with illness or hardship or some other life crisis.

What did I do with my newfound freedom? I started an English-language school that operated during the day in a popular night-club right beside Prague's Charles Bridge. We taught artists from the National Opera and budding young professionals who wanted to work with the influx of Western companies. Then I started an import-export business between India and Prague and opened a retail store. I'd never taught English before and I'd never worked in retail, let alone done buying for a store. In other words, I had no idea what I was getting myself into. I just caught the exuberant bug of the times, in a region of the world emerging from totalitarianism.

Then one day someone asked me, "Why are you doing all this here instead of in your own country?" That started me wondering how I could create the same kind of environment in Canada or the United States, where you were supposed to be free but didn't necessarily feel that way. We're all locked inside our heads, stuck in our limiting beliefs. Our "tanks" are internal. So ever since then, this has been a guiding question for me: "How do you get the tanks out of your head?" It led me to return to North America to create a number of businesses and become a mentor and advocate for entrepreneurs.

WHY SheEO?

I've mentored young entrepreneurs for over twenty years now. I love working with people who have youthful exuberance and passion. And it's not just a matter of being young—exuberance and passion can be found in all ages and demographics. I'm a dreamer myself, so it keeps me feeling fresh and on top of the latest trends and patterns to be sur-rounded by those who are curious and creating the future.

I started SheEO because I noticed that women were asking me questions that were quite different from men's. A lot of these questions revolved around the so-called soft skills—relationships, network building, and quality of life: "How do you deal with balance, with fear, with confidence?" "How do you build your network?" Men don't ask me these questions, even though I know they have them.

For years I kind of ignored the insight that lay in these questions. I knew it was there, but there was no way I'd admit that it's hard for women to balance so much, that we've been brought up differently, that we don't tend to have the kind of brash confidence so often rewarded in men. But of course it's true. Here's just one finding that proves the point: according to Global Entrepreneurship Monitor's 2012 *Women's Report*, women in every single economy included in the study have a lower perception of their capabilities and a greater fear of failure than men. I could ignore that reality for only so long. When a company I co-founded went public, I found myself looking at a pile of business plans that had been submitted for funding. Out of the four hundred applications, only *four* were from women. I knew I needed to do something about that.

So, in 2000, Kim Parlee and a few other women in our company created the SheEO Business Idea Competition, a $250,000 investment for young women under thirty with a plan for an internet business. It was funded by five women who each wrote a check for $50,000. We had a really hard time finding women entrepreneurs to apply. The pipeline wasn't there at the time, and it still isn't. Why? It's something that I couldn't put my finger on, and that I thought about off and on for a decade.

Thirteen years later, the SheEO question came back and struck me hard. I'd been an adviser at a government-funded innovation center in Toronto where less than 5 percent of its entrepreneurs were women. And I'd been mentoring many young, high-potential women entrepreneurs who were getting turned into pretzels by the startup game we've all agreed to play. It just wasn't working for them. They were bold, smart, sensationally talented young women who were trying to fit into the male-dominated, eat-your-neighbor, win–lose model. For one thing, that model is heavily biased against women. Many young men who don't even have a prototype will happily stand onstage at a pitch and talk about how they're going to disrupt an entire sector. It's this ballsy approach that investors so often value. But only for young men. If a woman walks in and pitches this way, investors will often eviscerate her, calling into question what her experience is and why she thinks she can do it.

Don't just take my word for it. Here are a few facts: Dow Jones VentureSource reported that in 2009 only 11 percent of U.S. firms with venture-capital funding had female CEOs. And it hasn't gotten a whole lot better since then. In 2012, only six out of sixty-six companies supported by the prestigious Y Combinator that year were run by women—and this despite research showing that women-run businesses are a better bet. According to the Small Business Administration's Office of Advocacy, venture capital firms that invest in women-led companies outperform those that don't. In Canada, the majority of government funding for startups through the FedDev program goes to men because someone decided that the only people worth supporting were STEM (science, technology, engineering, and math) grads—80 percent of whom are male. And things don't improve on the other side of the equation—in 2013 *Forbes* reported that, according to the Center for Venture Research, only 22 percent of angel investors are women (a 50 percent increase between 2011 and 2012). Somehow, women, whose collective population is greater than that of China and India combined and who make 85 percent of purchasing decisions, are considered a niche market in the startup game. The same *Forbes* article cited that, according to Babson College, if women were funded to the same degree as men, six million jobs would be created in five years.

Thought leaders, governments, and think tanks have for years been "trying" to change the ratio and increase the number of women in key leadership positions in every part of society. We've had a full-court press, or so it appears, to bring women to the table, but there's still an enormous disparity. Why is that?

I think it's because women don't want to play this game—a game that's created a huge gap between rich and poor, removed humanity from the equation, and led to the pursuit of profits at the expense of individuals. It's meant an unsustainable pace of work where people have no time for their families, much less themselves. So for those who realize they have a choice, the best path forward is to create opportunities on their own terms. "Leaning in" to a broken system is the last thing SheEOs want to do. Why are so many women starting businesses? Two of the most cited reasons are the desire for flexibility in the face of an untenable work–life balance and workplace gender discrimination. Why try to swim against the tide when you can jump into a whole new ocean? Breaking free to a whole new way of being, creating, making, and entrepreneuring is the new way forward.

This movement has been afoot for some time, but we've been so busy looking at the big trees in the forest that we've missed the developing undergrowth. According to a 2012 LexisNexis Global study cited in *Harvard Business Review*, the number of mentions of women entrepreneurs in the global press increased from about a hundred in 2002 to almost twelve hundred in 2012. Most global corporations have programs supporting women entrepreneurs as part of their strategy. A recent Global Entrepreneurship Monitor study found that in the United States, by 2018 the number of businesses started by women is expected to be *twice* that of men. Women own almost one-third of privately held companies, and one in five firms with revenue of at least $1 million was started by a woman, according to the National Women's Business Council. In Canada, the past fifteen years have seen a 50 percent increase in self-employed women. Globally, 126 million women started or were running new businesses in 2012, with women-owned businesses comprising about 37 percent of enterprises around the world. A lot of these businesses are small; 82 percent of them bring in less than $5 million a year in revenue. That's part of the recognition problem—society hasn't seen the contribution of women-led firms because they're not, on average, big.

But small is the new big. In a networked world, small wins every time. Small teams of talented people are the ones coming up with the new breakthrough ideas, not the big companies with tens of thousands of employees. Big companies are glacial and bureaucratic. Every big company in the world is trying to figure out how to be flexible and stay relevant. But how much longer can these companies continue paying a management tax when their new competitors have flatter organizations? Small is nimble. Small is adaptable.

And increasingly, big is in trouble. Big companies struggle to attract and retain talent. According to The Intelligence Group, 72 percent of millennials in the United States want to work for small companies or start their own; small startup companies have lineups at their door of young people wanting to work for them. And by 2025, millennials will be making up 75 percent of the workforce.

The old definitions of entrepreneurial success—going global, IPO-ing, making billions of dollars in revenue—are being replaced by a vision of happy, healthy workplaces that bring back humanity and create real value to real people in real communities. A majority of the North American economy is run by small businesses that have total control to create work environments on their own terms, in their own communities, and according to their own values. And it's not just happening in the U.S. and Canada. Today we're seeing the emergence of what venture capitalist Scott Hartley calls the "global entrepreneurial class, an identity that transgresses borders, nationalities, and religion. Entrepreneurs are a demographic, not a geographic, and their conspicuous creation is driving positive change in our world."

And it's women who are leading the parade of small businesses that will scale and connect in a networked world. Change is in the air. Women are more capital-efficient. Women reinvest in their communities. North American women make 85 percent of consumer buying decisions. As Cindy Gallop says, "Men are the niche market these days." In a 2013 article in *Fortune*, Warren Buffett declared that women are undervalued: "We've seen what can be accomplished when we use 50% of our human capacity. If you visualize what 100% can do, you'll join me as an unbridled optimist about [the] future."

Here are some examples of SheEOs out there building this future, now:

KACY QUA is redefining experiential education with Qualifyor.

HOLLY RUXIN is redefining wealth management with Montcalm TCR.

AYELET BARON is redefining the workplace with Simplifying Work.

CINDY GALLOP is redefining sex in the digital age with makelovenotporn.tv.

HEATHER PAYNE is redefining how women learn code.

JANE MCGONIGAL is redefining gaming to solve real-world challenges with Gameful.

SUZANNE BEIGEL is redefining how we finance ventures with collaboratewomenandgirls.com.

JOY ANDERSON is redefining how we create value in our systems with (re)Value.

OPRAH is redefining what it means to follow your bliss.

BEA ARTHUR is redefining psychotherapy in the digital age with Pretty Padded Room.

VANDANA SHIVA is redefining globalization.

BEYONCÉ is redefining stardom.

JANE WU is redefining how universities communicate with small donors with donoriq.

SHERENE NG is redefining dignity for the visually impaired with Adapative Designers.

LADY GAGA is redefining what it means to be different in this world.

SheEOs create from a more holistic view, a more feminine perspective that embraces relationships as the core element of every interaction in society. We are not machines. We are humans in a world full of love, sadness, hope, compassion, depression, hurt, and joy. Our businesses, institutions, and systems need to reflect our humanity. For the past too many centuries we've followed a mechanistic model. And we've suffered because of it. It's time to change the game.

MY DREAM FOR SheEO

I see SheEO as a network of networks that is huge in its impact. Women own 40 percent of businesses in the U.S., which are growing at twice the rate of businesses as a whole, and make 85 percent of buying decisions in North America. We have all that we need to support one another, finance one another, and create a whole new way of thriving on this planet. I envision cohorts of women funders, advisers, and supporters getting behind great creators, makers, and entrepreneurs and supporting them on their own terms. This will require a new financing model, a new education/learning model, and a new media approach. And it will be a collaborative effort of people around the world who decide that it's time for a change.

To support this worldwide transformation, I resurrected the SheEO program so that I could help women-led ventures clarify for themselves the impact they want to have in the world. That's because I believe that the most powerful leaders know what they truly want, know what they're good at, and know who they need to surround themselves with to build a great team. Most mentorship programs create a curriculum that follows a packaged approach to business: *Day One: Financials. Day Two: Legal. Day Three: Marketing, PR.* You won't find that approach at SheEO. We mentor and guide young entrepreneurs on their own terms.

It's also why I wrote this book. I know there's no single success model out there. I believe you can achieve greatness on your own terms, in a way that can help you thrive personally and professionally. Trying to fit yourself into someone else's model is a recipe for disaster. That's why SheEO aims to help you notice when you're doing that and to build up strategies to get you out of limited thinking and following voices that are not your own.

Finally, I believe in self-selection. If this message resonates, then this book is for you. It will take you through the eight SheEO principles I've cultivated by acting and learning, growing and stretching, failing, picking myself up, and persisting. And because I believe in Principle 8—that we're living in a post-hero world—I didn't want to do this book alone. That's why, as soon as I decided I had to write it, I called on my friend and colleague M.J. Ryan. M.J. is a masterful coach of entrepreneurs and executives. Her ability to help people source their greatness and then keep them on track is unparalleled. On top of that, M.J. is a book editor and best-selling author.

I've also learned from some of the wisest elders on the planet and have been privileged to be part of some incredible conferences and gatherings, including the World Economic Forum in Davos, the Tallberg Forum in Sweden, and the Clinton Global Initiative in New York. For most of my life I've been experimenting, building businesses, and challenging my and others' assumptions in order to find out what works for me. Slowly but surely I've been finding my tribe, people who resonate with the message of this book. The timing feels right now to launch this book and this movement because I've been receiving so many messages from so many of you.

I hope that exploring your leadership style and personal motivation will take you on a path to finding the business you and only you were meant to create. I offer principles, not rules, because there's no one right way of doing things. Principles are underlying truths that help create our mindset, and the SheEO movement is all about creating a new mindset and helping you find your own way: to walk your own path, blaze your own trail, and design an organization and a life that's worth living in the broader context of society.

Red Burns, who founded New York University's Interactive Tele-communications Program at Tisch School of the Arts, recently passed away at the age of eighty-eight. She was a huge influence on thousands of students over the years and won many accolades during her life. At the beginning of each school year she'd give a speech to her new students. I'm including lines from it here because it perfectly expresses my wishes for you as you embark on your SheEO journey.

WHAT I HOPE FOR YOU:

That you combine that edgy mixture of self-confidence and doubt

That you think of technology as a verb—not a noun; it is a subtle but important difference

That you remember the issues are usually not technical

That you communicate emotion

That you create images that might take a writer ten pages to write

That you look for the question, not the solution

That you are not seduced by speed and power

That you don't see the world as a market but rather as a place that people live in; you are designing for people—not machines

That you develop a practice founded in critical reflection

That you build a bridge between theory and practice

That you embrace the unexpected

That you listen … and ask questions

That you play

That you collaborate

That you turn your thinking upside down

That you understand what looks easy is hard

That you develop a moral compass

That you engage and have a wonderful time

A quick look out the window and it's clear that
we need to redefine, redesign, and recreate almost
every aspect of society.
#IamASheEO

SheEOs are women who leverage passions and
strengths to create businesses that build new models,
new mindsets, + new solutions.
#IamASheEO

In the distributed, networked world, it's the
creators, makers, and entrepreneurs that are the fuel
to get us to a better future.
#IamASheEO

For those who realize they have a choice, the best
path forward is creating on your own terms.
#IamASheEO

Breaking free to a whole new way of being, creating,
making, and entrepreneuring is the new way forward.
#IamASheEO

Small is the new big.
#IamASheEO

It's women who are leading the parade of
small businesses that will scale and connect in
a networked world.
#IamASheEO

PRINCIPLE

PRINCIPLE **1**

EVERYTHING IS BROKEN... WHAT A GREAT TIME TO BE ALIVE!

The reality is that we—all of us, not just the financial elite—are the collective sleepwalkers. How do we wake up? Why is it that, across so many major systems, we collectively create results that nobody wants?

—Otto Scharmer

Aihui Ong combined her passions for food and technology to build a platform called LovewithFood that connects food producers and consumers. It's a subscription service that delivers healthy organic snacks to customers each month and then donates a healthy meal at a food shelter for every box shipped. Her business is thriving, and creates a win–win–win for consumers, producers, and those who can't afford healthy food. But Aihui didn't stop there: she also built a revenue stream from corporations. For big brands that want to move into healthier snacks, LovewithFood customers provide a ready-made focus group whose insights these corporations are willing to pay for. I first heard about LovewithFood from Freada Kapor Klein, who's well-known for her impact investing and her belief that any business can have social impact. She invests only in businesses that actively close gaps, including achievement gaps in education, health-disparity gaps, and access-to-capital gaps.

Aihui and Freada are examples of SheEO Principle 1—that everything is broken and so it's a great time to be alive—meaning that it's precisely because we face enormous challenges that we have equally enormous opportunities for making a meaningful impact. Almost everything—from government to schools to businesses—needs to be fixed, redesigned, and rethought completely. And we aren't talking about little tweaks. We're talking about fundamental redesign. Quantum change. And that requires a new mindset and a new way of thinking. Sounds tragic? Terrifying?

If you, like Aihui and Freada, are a creator, maker, or entrepreneur, this is our nirvana. This is our moment. The world needs us—our fresh thinking, our disruptive ideas, our not just out-of-the-box but smash-the-box thinking. That's why it's such a great time to be alive! What we have to contribute has never mattered more. We need to stop listening to those voices that tell us "This is the way it should be" and just get on with experimenting with what feels right. Research on entrepreneurs reveals that we have seven common core traits: passion, tenacity, self-belief, flexibility, tolerance of ambiguity, rule breaking, and vision. This last quality—the ability to spot opportunities and imagine something that hasn't existed before—is what this chapter is all about. I believe that it's a mindset you can cultivate—and when you do, the world as it exists now goes from scary to thrilling.

I was recently at a talk given by Neil Turok of the Perimeter Institute, one of the preeminent centers for the study of theoretical physics. Neil remarked that, with all the data coming in from the Large Hadron Collider and the Planck Telescope, this is one of the most exciting times to be in physics. What physicists are finding is that there's an incongruity between the complexity of their theories and the simplicity of the emerging data. Our science needs to be every bit as beautiful as the evidence it points to, and the universe is revealing itself to us in new ways. It's telling us that our old theories need to be revised. Our computers are based on 1s and 0s, but that's not really how nature works. As humans we haven't evolved, yet, to experience things at the quantum level. But with these new tools available to physicists around the world, we're becoming able to simulate how the world works in order to help us see things differently.

How cool is that? And physics isn't the only realm returning information that reveals our lack of understanding and the need for innovation.

Take education, for instance. Richard Elmore, the Harvard education guru, says that the classroom and the public school are designed point by point to be exactly the opposite of what the latest neuroscience research is uncovering about how humans learn. Considering how much money is spent on education in each country, this spells huge business opportunities.

Or how about health care? The United States spends one-third of its health care budget in the last year of a person's life. Again, think of all the opportunities that exist to create solutions to that unsustainable fact.

Just a few more facts:

- Ninety percent of the weapons in the world right now are being sold, traded, and manufactured by the five permanent members of the Security Council. It's a great irony. We call it the Security Council, but it's the number-one dealer of weapons in the world. We can change that.

- We have to pay money to deposit our own money into our bank account. Really? How much longer do you think that's going to last?

- According to Edward Humes's 2012 book, *Garbology: Our Dirty Love Affair with Trash*, each person in the U.S. generates seven pounds of trash per day, and 69 percent of that trash goes immediately into landfills.

- According to the United Nations' 2006 *UN-Habitat* report, one-sixth of the world's population lives in shantytowns, considered breeding grounds for such social problems as crime, drug addiction, alcoholism, poverty, and unemployment.

- Astronomers don't know what 95 percent of the universe is made of. Atoms represent 5 percent, with dark matter and dark energy comprising the other 95 percent, and we don't yet know what they are.

- The world's eighty-five richest people have accumulated the same wealth as the world's 3.5 *billion* poorest people.

When I hear these examples I think, opportunity! It's disruption time. If you've got an idea for how to reform education, astronomy, mathematics, logistics, banking, waste management, or almost anything else, now's the time. How exciting and important is that!

I didn't used to feel this way. When I was in school, it seemed to me that everything was already figured out and all we needed to do was memorize the equation or learn the method and then go and apply it. There were set ways of doing things, authority still reigned supreme, and people generally trusted the authority around them. When I considered doing a PhD, I wondered how I could possibly come up with something totally new to research. But when I think about it now, I could do a PhD in a *lot* of topics. It's become pretty clear that we don't really know how most things work.

Our systems are stuck. The problems we're facing have moved beyond the institutions we've set up to deal with them. Experts tell us that everything is interconnected, and so as long as we operate in silos, we won't get where we need to go. I often hear the word *interconnected* and have often used it myself. *Interconnected. Interdependent.* But it wasn't until I heard Neil Turok talk about entanglement that I really got it. The word *interconnected* feels anemic to me. But the word *entanglement* takes me to a whole other level of thinking. I can't get away from you just as much as you can't get away from me. We're dependent on each other to get out of this mess. I need you and you need me. And we need our best, most creative thinking.

When I was at the 2013 Tallberg Forum in Sweden this past summer, I attended a session on youth unemployment in Europe. The experts in the group listed statistic after statistic on how bad things are and how they aren't going to get any better. One of the areas that had everyone stumped was job creation. A top European labor economist couldn't get beyond a "What if these jobs aren't coming back?" state of paralysis.

But rather than get caught in that fear, what if we use this reality to think big? Consider Jeremy Rifkin's big idea, which points to the possibility for true transformation. What if the intersection of 3D printing and an energy revolution, he wonders, allows us to have a very different future—where we can print whatever we need, even food, and where a networked solar and wind energy regime gets us off fossil fuels? Europe is already heading in that direction. It could be a whole new model for how to live on this planet. If we allocated our resources toward a new vision of a world that's far more human and holistic and far less machine, man-over-nature focused, imagine what could be possible. We need a lot more fresh-thinking, big-dreaming, open-minded, assumption-challenging people out there creating a new world.

In sector after sector, we're pretty clear on how we're in crisis. And yet the word for crisis in Chinese also means opportunity. Underlining SheEO Principle 1 is the commitment to see opportunities where others see crisis. We have a multitrillion-dollar liability in water infrastructure in North America and a global clean-water crisis. We have bankrupt cities and communities. We have unsustainable pension commitments. In many cities our urban transportation challenges are critical. The vast majority of our megacities are in the developing world, and according to a 2012 McKinsey Global Institute report, the 440 big cities in emerging economies will make up half the planet's economic growth by 2025. All of these challenges mean that tremendous opportunities are being created as well.

And, in those cases where we're clear about what we need to do, we have systems in place that seem to stop us from acting. My good friend, the scientist Bob Corell, has taken about 25 percent of U.S. senators up to the Arctic to see the melting ice, showing them in real time what we're doing to the planet. Every one of them gets it, he says, and each understands what needs to be done. Some, however, know that if they were to address the climate issue they'd not only likely be opposed by their more conservative colleagues, they wouldn't likely be re-elected. The politics of the Republican Party works against them, since acting on climate change and its causes aren't part of the party's platform.

Joi Ito from the MIT media lab feels that someone who writes a song has more power today than someone who's running a country: you can get your message out, it can spread like wildfire around the world in seconds, and people can change their mind in an instant and take action on it. But when you provide stacks and stacks of papers with consensus from the scientific community on the effects of climate change, no political system will act on it because the system is broken. The rules of the game are so entrenched that even reason, science, and truth can't break down the doors. And yet Beyoncé puts up her "Run the World (Girls)" video on YouTube and 212 million people, to date, have watched it. A generation of girls and boys are coming along with the words, images, and sounds of that video in their memory. What can you or I do with such potential for impact?

In many developed countries around the world, education and health care make up about 70 percent of the national budget. These two budget items will bankrupt every country that has an aging population. There's broad agreement on that fact, but it seems as if no one's really doing anything about it. We have political structures in place guaranteeing that no politician will act in the long-term interest of society because he or she isn't incentivized to do so. With two- to four-year election cycles, they measure success on the basis of re-election.

I was on a plane once with Peter Nicholson, the former head of strategy for Bell Canada, who said to me, "If there's a problem with the behavior, look at the incentive system." In most cases, our incentives are out of kilter with our desired results.

A lot of these systems-level issues require more than one bright entrepreneur, the old "hero" model, coming up with a solution. It's going to take a village to solve a lot of our challenges. Most of the meaningful opportunities to build social and financial value, to create positive change, and to make a difference won't be singular acts of heroism. In our entangled system, it will take key players coming together and collaborating to build value.

That's why the time is now for SheEOs. SheEOs understand, as Principle 8 says, that it's a post-hero world, that we can't go it alone. SheEOs work together, in peer-to-peer networks that support and leverage one another, to think and create bigger than any one of us could on our own. We understand the power of banding together to bring forward more options for action. And we understand that we can't make meaningful change if women's perspectives aren't included in the solutions.

Take Maria Antonakos, for instance. She's been building a global network of influencers to ensure that the Perimeter Institute can attract and retain the best female theoretical physicists in the world. "Virtually every modern technology—computers, electronics, wireless, GPS, lasers, medical and digital imaging, climate science, and more—is rooted in theoretical physics," she explains. "What's more, every one of those breakthroughs has rippled right across the sciences, catalyzing new discoveries. James Crick's background in quantum mechanics and x-ray crystallography, for example, helped make the discovery of DNA possible. Theoretical physics is the most efficient way to build a better, smarter, more prosperous world." As Maria says, "We know that to be the best in the world we need the best men and the best women."

FIVE PROMISING NEW TRENDS

Alongside the challenges we're facing, a number of new trends are emerging that make this time in history particularly exciting for SheEOs. Let's take a look at five of the most significant.

1. THE IDEA ECONOMY

In 1995, Roger Hendrix and Rob Brazell wrote a book called *The Idea Economy*. In it, they argue that the worldwide economy was shifting away from one in which people are employed by a business to implement someone else's idea to one in which people will be paid for creating an idea and implementing it themselves in some form. Ultimately, the authors argue, "There will be no job descriptions, just opportunities for ideas." Those who have the ability to create new ideas will have an advantage, they explain, because they can always generate more.

If we're indeed headed in this direction—and it certainly seems so, what with the decline of job security and the rise of freelancers and entrepreneurs—SheEOs are perfectly placed to thrive in this world where ideas are king.

2. THE LONG TAIL IS THE SheEO'S BEST FRIEND

The *long tail* is a statistical term. But in 2004, Chris Anderson used it in a *Wired* magazine article to describe the retail strategy of selling a large number of unique items in relatively small quantities rather than large quantities of a few items. He subsequently wrote a book on the topic, applying the theory more broadly to show how, especially given the easy access to markets through the internet, the economy is shifting "from mass markets to millions of niches." Anderson isn't the only one who's written about this. In a 2010 *McKinsey Quarterly* article, Shoshana Zuboff argued that the global economy is going through a transformation from mass consumption to the wants of individuals, in what she called "distributed capitalism." Examples include all the product customization we've seen in the past few years—for instance, jeans that are made specifically for you.

This transformation has massive implications for SheEOs. It means that you don't have to find a huge market for your offering—just the exact people who want what you have. It also means that your product needs to be different from everything else. The more differentiated you are, the more likely it is that people who want exactly what you're offering will want what you have. If you're trying to sell general books online, good luck: you're competing with millions. But if you specialize in books that aren't available on any other site, like certain technical works, then everyone who needs them will come to you. The market is small, but if it's big enough, you can capture it all and do well.

This new reality has created millions of opportunities for niche products and niche businesses. You don't have to create the next Apple. You just have to find your niche.

3. SOFTWARE IS EATING THE WORLD

Marc Andreesen coined this phrase to underline the fact that software is transforming many industries, and that if it hasn't come to you yet, it'll be arriving soon to eat your lunch. Netflix gobbled up Blockbuster. Amazon decimated Borders, and won't be happy till you buy everything from them, not just books. Disney had to buy Pixar to remain relevant. Software is the key to success for Walmart (logistics) and for FedEx. LinkedIn is the fastest-growing recruiting company. Financial services are feeling the disruption from PayPal and Square and Google Wallet, to name just a few companies vying to make banks as we know them a thing of the past.

This, too, is good news for creators, makers, and entrepreneurs. We can take part in the changes that such disruptions engender. As I mentioned, two huge areas that haven't yet felt the pressure from software are education and health care. But it's starting. Education-technology funding is on the rise. And it's clear that in the next two decades technology will play a major role in reinventing not only education but health care as well. If you've got a passion for either, this is a huge opportunity. And, not coincidentally, these are the two fastest-growing sectors for women entrepreneurs. According to *Growing Under the Radar*, a global 2012 study commissioned by American Express, women-owned firms with over $10 million in revenue grew 56.5 percent last year, which is twice the growth rate for all women-owned firms.

I've been working with many ed-tech startups in the past eighteen months and have witnessed the beginning of a sea change in how and where learning happens and how and when we pay for it. Sal Khan's Khan Academy aims for a free world-class education for anyone, anywhere. Heather Payne is a SheEO who started Ladies Learning Code and has now launched HackerYou, a condensed program that takes participants from novices to junior software developers in just nine weeks. There are thousands of these types of innovations now coming our way. Education delivery will never be the same.

Many are predicting the global demise of the university as we experiment with alternative means of accreditation. After all, it doesn't seem to make sense to have twenty thousand Introduction to Economics professors worldwide when you can take an online class from the best teacher in the world, virtually for free. The Gates Foundation spends millions of dollars each year to figure out the future of accreditation, with leading examples like Mozilla's Open Badge initiative. As Matt Gray from Bitmaker Labs declared in a *Financial Post* article, "No one cares about pieces of paper anymore." Well, some people do, but it's going to matter less and less.

When people can access free courses online and learn from the best teachers, everything changes. Tom VanderArk, former executive director of the education program at the Bill and Melinda Gates Foundation, partner at Learn Capital, and author of *Getting Smart: How Digital Learning Is Changing the World*, tells the story of a crowdsourcing campaign to create the best test-marking systems online. Hewlett-Packard crowdsourced the contest over six weeks, and there were three winners—one was from Quito, Ecuador; another was a Frenchman from Singapore; and the third was a teacher's assistant from Slovenia. It took these three people six weeks to beat the best-scoring companies in the world. What did they have in common? Each had taken Andrew Ng's online artificial intelligence course from Stanford. So no matter where you are and who you are, as courses head online taught by the best of the best, in most cases for free, barriers to learning are beginning to break down.

Even employers are less concerned about where you graduated than what you can actually do. LinkedIn is trying to reverse-engineer itself with endorsements to get a sense of what you're good at. Having a degree in X from Y university doesn't really mean anything anymore. What are you good at? How would we know?

Deloitte hires about eighteen thousand people in the United States every year, and most of them have been on an internship first to see if there's a fit with the company. Companies end up retraining the talent they want to hire to fit their needs anyway. Reliance on a degree to "prove" hire-ability will continue to diminish, I believe. What does that mean for what you want to create?

4. NEW WAYS TO WORK

Most of the young graduates I've talked to have no desire to work in a big company. The idea of waiting your turn, paying your dues, and working in cubicles is in direct opposition to every other trend that millennials experience—immediate feedback on almost everything they do in their personal lives through technology, total personalization, instant recommendations and insights, and on-demand information 24/7.

I recently had lunch with a senior executive of a large corporation. As I was talking to her about entrepreneurism as a career choice, she said, "I think the single biggest contributing factor to the rise in entrepreneurism is Take Your Kids to Work Day. Every year I see six hundred kids walking into our building on that day, and I turn to my assistant and say, 'Well, here comes another six hundred kids who'll never work for this company.' Because when they see what we do, how we do it, and where we work, they can't imagine spending their lives that way!"

As I look at the world of work, I keep thinking about TopCoder, TaskRabbit, 99Designs, and a host of other digital services that break down jobs into tasks. It seems pretty clear to me that the old notion of jobs will be replaced by the new notion of tasks. TopCoder takes previously unruly jobs that require a team to deliver and breaks them down into separate tasks that individuals can tackle, each working in their mastery, and build their reputation on. Half a million coders are part of the TopCoder community. These companies are early pioneers in moving to a new world of work.

For Ayelet Baron, former Cisco executive and current founder of a company that helps to create new ways to work, "The future workplace will work like the making of a movie, where the best talent gets matched to a project. We'll be able to tap in to the best people who have the skills and capabilities we need to get the job done—the film crew, actors, director, producer, makeup artists, costume designer. By focusing on how social technologies can connect and create communities, for example, organizations can more easily streamline work and create two-way communication channels for employees, customers, and partners. Soon we'll be talking about connected work instead of the latest technology, tool, or app."

5. HACKATHONS, INCUBATORS, AND CROWDFUNDING

All kinds of new avenues are opening up to democratize opportunities for those with the ambition to create the future now. There are many new forums to find your tribe, get connected, locate co-founders, discover your passions, and create the things you were meant to work on during this one precious life.

Hacking is the mantra of the millennial generation. Hackathons are gatherings of people who are passionate about a topic area and gather to work for a day or even a week on a challenge of interest to them. There are hackathon creators whose whole business is to help you set up a hackathon (angelhack) and hackathon do-it-yourself sites (hackathon.io). There are hackathons for everything you can imagine, including fashion (#fashionhack), health (#hackinghealth), government (reinventnyc.gov), and products for girls (Nike). Companies and organizations like Salesforce, Facebook, Google, NASA, and the UN have even launched their own hackathons. And there are hackathon portals that help you to see which hackathons are happening this week in your city. These are great places to find co-founders, learn more about an area of personal passion, and begin to build your networks around a topic you care about within a community.

Another growing trend to support entrepreneurs is incubators, also known as accelerators. They help startups get to market more quickly by providing advice, strategy, and basic services like legal and financial. Some even have funds to get you started up. The rise of incubators has been significant—there are thousands of them across North America, and at last count, twenty-three hundred in the U.S. alone. But these programs are of varying quality, so if you're considering applying to one, it makes sense to do your research.

The ways in which entrepreneurs are getting funded are also changing. Crowdfunding is a whole new way of raising capital for your business. It takes advantage of the internet to source people who like your idea and want to help fund it. It's a long-tail strategy—you get a little bit of money from a lot of people. There are perk-based crowd-funding sites like Kickstarter and Indiegogo where you don't give away any part of your business and you raise money by pre-selling items or giving people perks. Others charge a percentage of money raised.

Crowdfunding is accelerating at an unprecedented rate. It's affec-cting government policy, informing enterprise innovation, and changing the role of financial institutions around the world. According to the *2013CF Crowdfunding Industry Report*, in 2012 crowdfunding grew by 81 percent to $2.7 billion invested and was projected to reach $5 billion in 2013. Social causes are the most active, driving 30 percent of all crowdfunding activity, followed by business and entrepreneur-ship, and finally by energy and environment. Donation or perk-based crowdfunding is up 85 percent ($1.4 billion), lending-based funding is up 111 percent ($1.2 billion), and equity-based crowdfunding is up 30 percent ($116 million). Five years ago, this type of financing hadn't even been invented.

Crowdfunding sites like Portfolia and Fundable provide equity financing, and in the near term, regulators in the United States and Canada will rule on how these new financing methods can scale. It's pretty clear that we're in the very early stages of financing reform. In the next decade the number of places open to entrepreneurs to get their seed and growth financing is likely to explode with new possibili-ties. Our new networked world will see thousands of opportunities for people to aggregate their capital and get behind entrepreneurs, sec-tors, or challenges they want to support in whole new ways.

People are increasingly talking about having philanthropic and equity mash-ups to finance long-term approaches to systemic transfor-mation. This requires a change in thinking, from donation/investment to impact: "Is this organization creating the kind of impact I want to contribute to?" Instead of using the old donation-versus-investment construct, we need a model that focuses more on impact and how we can deploy capital in new ways. We don't need any more either/ors; we need and-and-and approaches. This is something I'm very excited about, as I plan to build up a fund to finance SheEOs with a new approach that takes into account social and financial impact.

As I look ten years into the future, I feel that there'll be many more of these places offering support. There won't be only one game in town.

If you're a creator, a maker, or an entrepreneur who wants to build something of value, you'll have a multitude of places to get support, advice, and financing from people who get what you're doing in ways that suit your needs and your values. That's one of the many reasons why it's the perfect time to be a SheEO.

Because we face enormous challenges,
there are equally enormous opportunities
to have a meaningful impact.
#IamASheEO

The world needs us—our fresh thinking, our
disruptive ideas—our not just out-of-the-box but
smash-the-box thinking.
#IamASheEO

If we allocated our resources toward a new
vision of a world that was far more human and holistic,
imagine what could be possible.
#IamASheEO

I'm committed to seeing opportunities
where others see crisis.
#IamASheEO

SheEOs work together to support and
leverage one another, to think and create bigger
than any one of us could do on our own.
#IamASheEO

This new reality has created millions
of opportunities for niche products and
niche businesses. Find your niche.
#IamASheEO

PRINCIPLE **2**

MEANING IS THE NEW MONEY

What am I living for and what am I dying for
are the same question.

—Margaret Atwood, *The Year of the Flood*

About fifteen years ago, I was at the World Economic Forum's annual conference with the Global Leaders for Tomorrow network when our keynote speaker, Hillary Clinton, walked up to the podium. I'll never forget her opening line: "I was asked to come and speak to you today about leadership, but my first question is, leadership for what?" I could see half of the audience wondering, "What's she talking about? I don't get it; I'm on a path to the top of my company," and the other half thinking, "That's exactly what I'm struggling with. I'm already number two at my Fortune 100 company and I'm thirty. Is this all there is? Why am I here? What is the point of my life?"

SheEO Principle 2—that meaning is the new money—encapsulates the fact that more than ever before, people are asking their version of Hillary Clinton's question. They want to know that their work has meaning. That it creates a positive impact. That it moves the needle on creating the kinds of changes the world needs.

All sorts of research back up this principle. For instance, PwC's 2012 *Millennials at Work* report—done for the financial services sector, which typically attracts young people highly motivated by money— found that, worldwide, millennials are "looking for more in life than 'just a job,' or a steady climb through the corporate ranks. They want to do something that feels worthwhile; they take into account the values of the company when considering a job...." And a recent Millennial Branding report found that the majority of people in this demographic—72 percent—seek work with greater meaning.

To meet this need, organizations like Escape the City have sprung up online. Founded by two young British management consultants for whom the corporate world was stultifying, Escape the City is "a global community for people who want to 'do something different' with their careers. We help talented people escape or avoid corporate jobs.... We believe there is more to life than doing work that doesn't matter to you." Similarly, Amanda Minuk's BMeaningful.com is "founded on the belief that there is more to life than a paycheck."

But it's not only young people who crave meaningful work. NetImpact's *What Workers Want in 2012* report surveyed 1726 currently employed Gen Xers, baby boomers, and millennials, as well as university students about to enter the workforce, who ranked "having a job where I can make an impact" as more important than a prestigious career, wealth, or being a community leader. As the hundreds of millions of baby boomers around the world reach retirement with an average of twenty-plus more years of life, they're asking themselves where they want to devote their energy, passion, and expertise in order to create a better world.

And it's women who are, by far, leading the way in this trend. In its study, NetImpact discovered that compared with about 40 percent of the men, 60 percent of the women polled, both students and the currently employed, said that working for a company that prioritizes social and environmental responsibility is very important to them. And 30 percent of working women said they'd be willing to take a 15 percent pay cut for a job with impact, compared with only 19 percent of men. "Women think about the future, and what sort of world is being created for future generations," remarks Theresa May, British Home Secretary and former U.K. Minister for Women and Equalities. In an article in the *San Francisco Chronicle* on the organization Tech-Women, which brings women from third world countries to Silicon Valley for networking and mentorship, LinkedIn executive Florina Xhabija commented on this female focus on making a difference: "The projects these women suggest—they're not like Instagram for dogs, they are trying to solve real issues." Rather than focusing on profit making and exit strategies, as many male entrepreneurs do, women tend to focus on finding meaningful solutions to real problems.

There are so many SheEOs out there doing amazing things. As just one example, I think of Debbie Sterling, the creator of GoldieBlox, a company that builds games for girls in order to inspire future engineers. Debbie didn't even know there was such a career as engineering until a high school math teacher suggested she might want to major in it in college. After graduating with a degree in mechanical engineering and product design, she looked at the fact that 89 percent of all engineers worldwide are men and felt determined to close that gender gap. "We believe," she writes on her website, "there are a million girls out there who are engineers. They just might not know it yet. We think GoldieBlox can show them the way."

The success of this two-year-old company shows how powerful meaning-based organizations can be. Launched through a wildly successful Kickstarter campaign, GoldieBlox now has products in Target, Toys R Us, and over a thousand mom-and-pop toy stores. GoldieBlox recently beat out twenty thousand other companies in a fan-voting contest sponsored by Intuit to score a free thirty-second ad during the Super Bowl, where half-minute spots typically go for $4 million.

While Debbie Sterling clearly found her calling, it's not as easy for many young women. In a recent conversation with a group of enthusiastic university students, I asked them what they were worried about. One young woman said, "I want to do something that the six-year-old me would be proud of." I was floored. What a brilliant insight and a beautiful desire. And yet, just in her second year, she felt she was being pushed away from that desire and pressured to pick the right, the accepted, the chosen path according to her peers and professors.

Fortunately, the desire for meaningful work, combined with the recognition of SheEO Principle 1 that everything is broken, has resulted in an upsurge of social entrepreneurs, women and men who are creating organizations with the aim of solving social problems or effecting social change through innovative solutions. Social entrepreneurship has exploded in the last ten years, going from an undefined term to a variety of programs offered at more than thirty-five business schools around the world. What exactly constitutes a social entrepreneur is still being debated, but they're typically defined by three things: they draw upon models from both the business and nonprofit world; they measure performance not only in profit and return but also in positive return to society; and they operate in all kinds of large and small organizations as nonprofits, for-profits, and hybrids.

For me, the point isn't how a social enterprise is defined, or whether the term is already passé, or whether you formally consider yourself a social entrepreneur. Regardless of whether or not you decide to structure your organization around the principles and practices of social entrepreneurship, I believe it's crucial that you get in touch with what gives meaning to your life and figure out how to build a business around that. Or if you already have a business, to make sure that it's aligned with what matters to you most. Meaning gives you the "why" of what you're doing, and in order to build a powerful "what," you need to first be in touch with that powerful "why."

WHY MEANING?

Getting in touch with what matters to you is important because starting and running a business take a lot of focus, energy, determination, and persistence. And it's a whole lot easier to keep your focus, find your energy, and be determined to keep on going when you believe wholeheartedly in what you're creating. When it matters deeply to you.

Meaning guides your choices and helps you navigate through all the complexities of life and business. It's different from a goal because it's not something that can be checked off a list as accomplished. Rather, it can be enacted in multiple ways throughout your lifetime. For instance, what's most meaningful to me is to maximize my impact on this planet. Everything I choose to do goes through that filter: "Will this maximize my impact?"

Meaning carries energy: "Nothing is going to stop me from doing this." And it's that kind of energy and intention you need to create a successful business. I've often sat in rooms where people were deciding what kind of organization to launch because they wanted to create something successful. I can only sit quietly for so long before I blurt out, "This can't be manufactured. If you're determined to change something, fix something, or right some wrong, then you have to do it. But if you're exploiting a market opportunity and missing the bigger picture of why you, why now, then good luck to you. Life is too short to be working on things to exploit." I believe very strongly in what Red Burns, the iconic founder of NYU's Interactive Technologies Program, said in the speech I quoted at the beginning of this book:

"What I hope for you ... is that you don't see the world as a market, but rather as a place that people live in—you are designing for people—not machines." What you're creating has to be in your sweet spot of meaning, or it's ultimately not worth doing.

Meaning is also powerful because it creates engagement, and engagement is key to success. That's why, when Gallup asked 1.7 million employees around the world about indicators of profitability and productivity, one of the top twelve was "The mission of my organization makes me feel like my work is important." This factor alone results in 15 to 30 percent less turnover. A clear sense of meaning binds people in an organization together, encourages them to work harder, and makes them want to stay. It's like the North Star, helping you understand where you're trying to go and to collectively aim yourselves in that direction.

Another way of looking at meaning is that it's your intrinsic motivation. And intrinsic motivation is needed to run successful businesses in today's world. Here's why: drawing on forty years of research, Daniel Pink reveals in his book *Drive* that external motivators—chiefly money—are good only for routine, non-creative tasks. They actually *inhibit* complex, creative, out-of-the-box thinking, which comprises most of the work the twenty-first century calls for. External motivators encourage a focus only on the short-term. Intrinsic motivators, on the other hand, encourage innovation, a wider focus, and better long-term thinking. Which do you want for you and your organization? Every successful social entrepreneur has embraced what Stanford political science professor Rob Reich calls "massive innovation." In order to do that, your individual and company drivers need to come from within.

So what are the intrinsic motivators of high performance? Pink describes three:

1. **Autonomy:** the drive to do it your own way

2. **Mastery:** the desire to learn and grow, and take on new challenges

3. **Purpose:** the deeply felt need to make a difference in the world

The desire for autonomy is behind much of the entrepreneurial impulse. You want to do it your way. In Principle 3, I'll discuss why you being you and doing it your way is absolutely critical.

Here we're focusing on the third motivator: meaning, also known as purpose. "Purpose provides activation energy for living," psychologist Mihaly Csikszentmihalyi is quoted as saying in *Drive*. I couldn't agree more. When we're on purpose, we're tapping in to an energy source that gets us up in the morning and gives us the creative juice to overcome obstacles. But we're not just tapping in to that energy source— when we're in touch with our sense of meaning, we're actually *creating* energy that draws other people and opportunities to us.

PULL VERSUS PUSH

When you're doing what truly matters to you, you're using a pull strategy. You don't have to push for what you want—it starts to come to you: opportunities, potential partners, and employees that align with your purpose. Customers or clients, too. That's because this increased longing for meaning is true for consumers as well as workers. The clearer you are about your purpose and the more you articulate it, the more you'll attract clients and customers who are aligned with that purpose. As Simon Sinek says in a popular TED talk, "People don't buy what you do, they buy why you do it."

Ultimately, the reason to create meaningful work is that it makes us happier. Here's just one research example. In a study of University of Rochester soon-to-be graduates, researchers found that they fell into two categories—those with what they called "profit goals" (to become wealthy or famous, for instance) and those with "purpose goals" (to help others, to improve the world in some way). After these graduates had been out of school for a couple of years, they were interviewed again. Those with purpose goals had higher levels of satisfaction and well-being and lower levels of anxiety and depression than they had when they were in college. Those with profit goals were no happier than they'd been in college and suffered from higher levels of depression and anxiety—even if they'd achieved their goals!

In short, a meaningful life is a more fulfilling one. Psychologists have discovered that a sense of meaning is not only associated with an increased sense of well-being, but it can also help you cope more successfully with life's challenges and stresses. Think of it as entrepreneur insurance!

FINDING MEANING

It's one thing to want to make an impact and quite another to figure out what kind of impact is right for you. In my role as a mentor, I meet hundreds of people who've done all kinds of interesting internships and volunteer experiences. They've checked the box. But many of these people don't have a sense of any deeper meaning guiding their choices. Of course, part of that is age. Looking back, it's easier to see a pattern. My entrepreneurial life is a great example of this pattern, but like anyone's, it wasn't as visible to me in the beginning as it is now. Now, when I write it down in this book, the pattern is clear. See for yourself: When I came back from Prague, obsessed with the question of how to create an environment where people go beyond what they thought was possible for them, I wondered where to start. To me the simplest place was with youth. Young people have fewer layers of the onion to peel, as it were. Since they don't know what's impossible, they're more likely to tackle impossible challenges and stretch themselves. So, I went to the largest school board in Canada and said that I wanted to create a new curriculum for young people that focused on entrepreneurship, global education, and technology. The idea was to place sixteen-year-olds in a company's corporate office to work on a digital project, after which the companies would send those youths overseas to their foreign office to do a one-month project. And I said that I'd cover my own salary by raising the money, a $6000 ask.

At the time, I'd been out of the country for almost five years and had no network to speak of in Toronto. I ended up making a thousand cold calls to companies, looking for sponsorship of the program. Coming off my Prague experience, I believed that anything was possible and was fearless in my pursuit. Well, until I got a *lot* of rejection. No one liked the idea. Many of my first calls were met with this kind of response: "Are you kidding me? I have a sixteen-year-old at home and there's no way I'd hire him/her to do anything." *Click.* At night I'd call my brother Mark, sometimes in tears of frustration, complaining that no one "got it"—a common whine of mine back in the early days of entrepreneuring—and he'd make me laugh with some hilarious joke. He not only distracted me from the hill I was climbing but also encouraged me to go on.

Then, one day, I called the federal government to ask for advice. My uncle had always said to me, "If you want money, ask for advice, and if you want advice, ask for money." I never truly understood the power of this approach until that day. As soon as I got the government official on the phone, I said, "I don't want money from you; I'm calling to ask for advice about a program I'm creating." There was silence on the other end. "You don't want money?" She sounded flabbergasted. Then we launched into a long conversation about the goals of the program, and my thesis—that getting experience as young as possible to do things no one else would hire you to do without a degree was critical to building entrepreneurial, risk-taking skills. She was very supportive of the idea. About two months later, I got a call out of the blue from the same office: the government was interested in piloting international internships, and did I want $150,000 in funding?

Eventually, I got the remainder of the funding from ten companies, selected the students, and hired a teacher. Then the placements began: the students went to countries around the world, and the teacher monitored them over the internet—and this was in 1995. It was an amazing experience. One student learned how to set up Lotus Notes in the Toronto office of the Royal Bank of Canada and then went to their London, U.K., office to set it up there and train everyone in how to use the software. When all kinds of success stories began to emerge from the program, I realized I was on to something. Don Tapscott began writing *Growing Up Digital* at the same time, and we both had stories attesting to a sea change: young people being skilled in an emerging new world that most adults didn't really understand.

Around the same time I met Richard Ford, who'd won the National Marshall McLuhan Award for Distinguished Teacher for inventing the first integrated arts program in Canada. According to Veronica Lacey, director of the North York Board of Education at the time and later Ontario's deputy minister of education, he was the "Van Gogh of teachers." I'll never forget the first day I walked into Richard's classroom. The kids were running the class. He saw his role as being the facilitator who dropped in challenges and then got out of the way as soon as possible so that the students could solve the problems themselves. I was blown away by the environment he'd created and the way he set kids up to achieve the impossible. I was hooked. He and I have collaborated personally (we're now married) and professionally ever since.

After we did a couple of pilot programs inside his high school, we realized that we wanted to create a company that hired youth to solve digital problems no one else could figure out. We called it KidsNRG.

The dot-com era was upon us, so our timing was perfect. Our first summer we hired fifty-four young people, between the ages of fourteen and twenty-four, to work on ten projects for companies and organizations ranging from Xerox and the Royal Bank of Canada to Tapscott's *Growing Up Digital* book launch, for which the students built the website and community tools. The stories that emerged, the learning that took place, and the products that were created were a perfect combination. Students lined up to work for our company, and many of Canada's top companies hired us to work on digital projects they couldn't solve. One client, Design Exchange, had spent over $100,000 trying to digitize the encyclopedia of design; everyone had told them it wasn't yet possible. They hired KidsNRG, and a sixteen-year-old named Sep Seyedi did it in six weeks, emailing senior Sun Java programmers at two a.m. asking for help, because he didn't know it was impossible and they had no idea he was sixteen.

As the stories grew and as students gain skills and networks and as products and solutions were created, many of the youth we worked with began to start their own businesses. From 1995 to 2000 we spun out over twenty businesses run by youth and raised millions of dollars to invest in their businesses. Then, in April 2000, we went public on the Toronto Stock Exchange with Canada's first public online incubator.

After KidsNRG, we created a consulting company called Impactanation. It was another iteration on the idea of bringing in the energy of young people to solve major challenges. We worked with a global oil services company to design a fund and a curriculum that called young people to action around creating solutions to water issues in their communities. We also worked on a project in which young people came up with innovative approaches to dealing with malaria in different countries.

Then we set up a fund to invest in young people's ideas for solutions to some of the intractable grand challenges we're facing. But as we worked with these young people, I began to see that the more they learned about the problems facing the planet, the more they felt too insignificant to solve them. The feeling was "What difference does my little contribution really make when six billion people are part of the problem?" That's when my interest in technology started re-emerging. I wondered, "What if there was a way of creating software to track the impact of individual actions and aggregate them? If I do these three things and my friends do these seven things, look at the impact we'd all have. And if it could be visualized, maybe we could see our impact and start to change our behaviors."

I started a software company called Zazengo so that people could get a sense of the difference their small changes made when added together with thousands of others. Our first client was Walmart, which used our platform to track its employees' personal sustainability plans.

With the launch of SheEO, you can see that I'm still working on the big question I uncovered in Prague, which is how to create experiences, environments, products, and tools for people to discover their potential, to reach beyond what they thought was possible, and to have a positive impact on the world.

DISCOVERING WHAT MATTERS TO YOU

No matter how young you are—even if you're in your twenties and this is your very first venture—you can get clearer on what matters to you. In fact, I still work on this regularly myself; it's a continual, lifelong practice. Ultimately, discovering what has meaning for you is a process of looking deeply into yourself and trying out what you're noticing so that over time you'll feel more and more aligned.

Finding and aligning with meaning takes boldness. It's risky to declare what truly matters to you, to put yourself out there for the world to see. But I want to really encourage you to take the risk. What else are you here for? Now let's look at some approaches to get you started.

1. CREATE A WORD CLOUD

Whenever someone comes to me for help getting clear on meaning, my mind immediately goes into question mode. So imagine we're having a conversation. Take out a piece of paper and make a word cloud of your answers to these questions:

- If anything was possible, what would you spend your time doing?
- What could you do all day long and never get tired of it?

- What seems broken to you? What do you want to fix?

- What people would you like to be surrounded by? What attributes do they have?

- What issues, ideas, people, and projects move you deeply?

- What is the one thing you've always dreamed of but are afraid to do?

- What did you dream of being when you were a child?

If you find yourself thinking, "Oh, but I could never do what I love," do the next practice as well.

2. FIND YOUR TRIBE

To get over your belief that something's not possible, how can you find people who are already doing what you don't believe you can do? Whenever I get stuck and wonder about what's possible as an entrepreneur or creator, I think of the thousands and thousands of people who are out there pursuing their passion. Have you ever driven by those industrial strip malls where you see hundreds of small units? I often think, "What are all these businesses doing? Who are these people and who are their customers and how did they get started? They're each doing something." There are millions of successful businesses out there, although you often have to look beyond the traditional magazines and media to find them.

This quote from dot-com pioneer Joe Kraus really resonated with me: "The twentieth century was about dozens of markets of millions of consumers. The twenty-first century is about millions of markets of dozens of consumers." It validated my belief in the multitude of possibilities to build something.

The whole world is available on the internet as your inspiration. Do a key-word search of all the things you're passionate about and watch what comes up so that you'll get a sense of the possibilities. Or type in three things you're passionate about along with "find a success story." Go to the impact section of *The Huffington Post* where they feature people across every sector doing cool stuff that makes a difference. Check out www.care2.org—it has over twenty-five million members dedicated to green, healthy living while making a difference. Look at www.ashoka.org, whose slogan is "innovators for the public." It's a network of thirty thousand social entrepreneurs and change makers around the world. Seeing what other people are doing can help you align what you love with what you want to create as a business. And these organizations also provide a great way for like-minded people to connect so that you won't have to necessarily go it alone.

3. WHAT'S YOUR SENTENCE?

This one comes from *Drive*. In it, Daniel Pink tells a story about Clare Booth Luce, a U.S. congresswoman and adviser to President John F. Kennedy. She was afraid that he had too many priorities and was therefore lacking focus. "A great man is one sentence," she told him. "Abraham Lincoln's sentence was 'He preserved the union and freed the slaves.' Franklin Roosevelt's was 'He lifted us out of a great depression and helped us win a world war.'" In order to get clarity around your purpose, it helps to think about what you want your sentence to be.

4. GET IN TOUCH WITH YOUR CORE VALUES

Meaning is also found in what you truly care about. Some people call that core values. Here's a way, from the Search Inside Yourself Institute, to get clearer on your own core values:

1. Write down the names of three people, living or dead, fictional or real, whom you admire greatly.

2. For each person, write down what qualities they have that you admire.

3. Now look at your answer for #2 and write down the list of your three to five core values, assuming that what you admire in another person is what you most highly value.

What can you create that expresses these values? How can what you're already creating express those values?

5. UNCOVER YOUR THEMES

What is it that you can't help doing—it just keeps showing up over and over in your life? You can see mine in my story about the organizations I've created. They're all about harnessing the energy of young people and creating maximum impact. I've tried every permutation and combination to hit these themes: launching a nonprofit, for-profits, a tech company, and a consultancy, and creating programs, engaging with universities and other educational venues, giving speeches, and serving as a mentor. Like everyone else, I can get bogged down in details or start to feel that I can't do it. That's when I say to Richard, "Let's just go live on a desert island." Then we laugh because we know that if we did we'd soon start organizing programs to engage youth and support entrepreneurship on the whole island. It's what we're here to do.

What are your themes? They're like a fire inside you. You just can't stop them, even if you choose to ignore them for a while. It might be hard to see them on your own. If so, find someone like a coach or mentor who's good at listening and hearing the pattern to help you draw it out. Trust that everything you've ever done isn't wasted, and in fact has brought you to this moment. It's part of the pattern of meaning in your life.

6. GET OUTSIDE YOURSELF

I learned this one from designer and developer Dave Hariri. He was three months into his supposed dream job when a friend offered him the chance to build a business he could design from the bottom up. To figure out what to do, he spoke to employers, friends, and family through the lens of what would be best for his development. He couldn't decide. Then he asked his father, who suggested that he think about it not in terms of his personal progress but rather which option would be better for the world's progress. "Once the context was outside myself," Dave said, "I quickly realized that the sooner I began contributing to fulfilling my intended purpose, the better."

If you look at what's showing up in your life and ask what's best for the world, what would you choose to do? I'm not saying you should do something you hate, but how can you align what's good for you with what's good for the world?

ORGANIZATIONAL MEANING

Once you're clear about what's meaningful to you personally, you need to make sure your organization has a strong purpose as well. In his book *Design-Driven Innovation*, Roberto Verganti writes, "People do not buy products but meanings." The same is true for services. When your product or service is grounded in a clearly articulated meaning, it guides everything you do—business development, marketing, product development, sales decisions.... It helps guide communications, priorities, actions, and responsibilities, and even how you work with others.

Typically, this meaning is captured in a mission statement—which tells you and the world why the organization exists. Even though many companies have long ones, great mission or purpose statements are short—fewer than twenty words is best. It should be clear, concise, inspiring, and memorable enough for you to remember. Here are a few great ones:

> **TED:** "Spreading ideas."
>
> **THE NATURE CONSERVANCY:** "To conserve the lands and waters on which all life depends."
>
> **GOOGLE:** "Organize the world's information and make it universally accessible and useful."
>
> **ZAPPOS:** "To provide the best customer service possible."

Notice how these are specific—they avoid generalities like "make a difference."

An easy way to get started is to fill in the following sentence: *The mission of [my organization] is to [verb] the [population served] through [core services and core values]*. If I were doing it for SheEO, for instance, I'd fill in the blanks like this: "The mission of the SheEO program is to mentor, guide, and accelerate the next generation of women-led ventures on their own terms." Accurate, yet not necessarily inspirational, right? Then work with that starting point and refine it until you feel a yes inside. If you have employees, include them in this process. Brainstorm on stickies (one word per sticky) the key words that describe what gives meaning to what you're doing. Find the common powerful themes, then fill in the blanks and refine the concept.

Once you've got something that excites and inspires you, brainstorm ways to use it on an ongoing basis. Post it on your website, place it on your letterhead and marketing materials, and use it to set company strategy and goals by asking yourself, "If this is our mission, what are our key priorities?" Make your reason for existence visible on a daily basis and find ways to use it to measure your performance as well.

With KidsNRG, our statement was "Imagine growing a youth-inspired global community where the possibilities are limitless." We used it for performance reviews, where we asked, "How are you imagining/being creative? Are you working closely with youth? Are you thinking globally? In a community manner? Are you limiting your thinking or staying in the possibilities?" In short, it's best if you can find something that's aspirational as well as measurable.

DEFINING SUCCESS ON YOUR OWN TERMS

When the SheEOs who've gone through the program provide feedback, one thing that gets mentioned consistently is how much we encourage women to define success on their own terms. This goes hand in hand with meaning for me, because only you get to determine what's meaningful for you and only you get to decide what a successful venture is *for you*.

A light bulb went off for SheEO Jane Wu when she first heard me make that statement. "I went to one of the best business schools in Canada. I got accepted as one of the top most entrepreneurial undergrads for a program called Next36. I've been lucky enough to have access to many resources and access to a big network of mentors and advisers," she explains. "But in the SheEO program, I heard something I'd never heard before. The way I've been trained to do business is burning the midnight oil and a male-defined status quo. When Vicki said I could redefine what success was to me, what it means in a holistic way, it was a holy #$% moment. All the programs I've been through are amazing, but they've shown me only one model of how to do it."

In the United States and Canada, the majority of the economy is made up of small businesses employing fewer than a hundred people. And yet the only models of success the media tends to celebrate are the Fortune 100s. Whether in coaching and mentoring, entrepreneurial education, or traditional incubators, the assumption is that you're going to go big. But if your definition of success is just the current game—to get X rounds of VC (venture capital) funding, scale it, and then do an IPO that makes you a billionaire—opportunities to reach that goal will be limited. This is also happening in the social entrepreneur world, where traditional business leaders are bringing their model into the social space, telling everyone that they need to scale up if they find something that's working. But I'd argue that this scale model isn't really working. So why should we follow that model when building our social- or impact-driven businesses?

If instead you're asking yourself, "What really matters to me? How can I create an organization that's just the right size and will have the impact I want?" then there are many more possibilities. Then you're creating your own game and redefining the rules of winning.

Just think of a few of the "rules" for "successful" entrepreneurs:

- You have to create a business that will scale.
- You should be thinking about your exit from day one.
- You start with angel financing and then move to VC funding.
- You have to work 24/7.

What if none of these rules were the case for you? What if you started with yourself and your idea and made enough money for you from the start? What if you want to have ten employees and make a decent living and define your hours and work close to home and bring your dog to work and work with people you love and don't want to grow bigger?

If so, there are infinite possibilities for you to be successful, happy, and have a company that does something meaningful. Here are three examples.

Kacy Qua left formal schooling in the eighth grade, bored with the curriculum and feeling as if the people who were successful in school weren't necessarily successful in life. Then she started to intern and loved it. She eventually returned to school, and later spent a few years working on incentivizing entrepreneurs to solve big challenges through the XPrize. That's when she began noticing antiquated systems. Recently, she founded Qualifyor in order to address the failings of an education system that doesn't prepare the next generation to live happy, healthy lives. She's working with the generation of unemployed, uninspired youth who have unique talents, connecting them to what they're passionate about and building their networks and experience by doing real work as part of their schooling. Funded by the Downtown Project in Las Vegas, Qualifyor is pioneering the future of education and training.

While Kacy is redesigning the experiential education system, Ayelet Baron is passionate about unleashing the superpowers of corporations around the world with her new company, Simplifying Work. This former head of Strategy for Cisco Canada is developing a diagnostic tool for leaders to assess whether their business is leading or stuck in the past based on six critical factors.

Bea Arthur decided to change the traditional therapeutic model by giving women access to therapists anytime and anywhere. She created Pretty Padded Room, an online platform that connects clients from all over the world with an all-female team of licensed therapists who provide direct support through video chat or a Digital Diary, written consultations that are assessed with feedback without an appointment. Women of all ages sign up to get help with stress management, couples counseling, job stress, life transitions, and a variety of other issues.

As you can see from these three examples, the opportunities for your creativity are endless. However, because we tend to have such a limited notion of success, it's crucial that you step back and think about what success means for you personally—emotionally, physically, mentally, spiritually, financially. Otherwise you'll end up creating someone else's organization and living someone else's life. Get as granular as you can, and don't limit your thinking to the existing possibilities presented to you. For instance, I work with a consultancy in Sweden that has one rule: they only work with nice people. You can imagine people saying that this isn't realistic. Well, what if it was? Working with people you want to work with on projects you want to work on is the only way for SheEOs. This is your life! In a world of seven billion people there's an abundance of everything, and so this Swedish consultancy has been able to find plenty of clients who fit their rule.

Assume you can have exactly what you want and then answer the following questions:

- What's your perfect workplace? What does it look like? Where is it? What are all the elements of this perfect workplace?

- Who are the kinds of people you want to work with?

- What kind of investors do you want to have? What are their attributes? Are they just there with money? Do they have connections? Are they coming with something you need as well as the money?

- Who are your dream customers and clients? What attributes do they have? Are there clients you wouldn't want? Can you create an algorithm to select who you want to work with and who you don't?

- What size of organization feels right for you?

- What kind of workplace norms do you want to create? A four-day workweek? No email on weekends? One-hour turn-around time on inquiries?

- How much money do you need to make?

Be specific and iterate the list often. I've noticed over time that I answer these questions differently as I get closer and closer to understanding what really works for me versus what I think I'm supposed to want.

We live in the age of total customization and personalization. You can go online and create your own running shoes, your own jeans, your own backpack. You get your customized email, your customized news, your customized searches. Yet when we talk about success, it's a cookie-cutter template. We assume that pursuit of money is the goal. That being the next billion-dollar company is the destination. Now, it may be that the pursuit of what's currently defined as success is right for you. Great! But if it's not, it's worth exploring what success *does* mean for you. You can create your own customized version of success—you just have to claim it.

OVERCOMING SELF-LIMITING BELIEFS

If you find that your mind keeps going to all the reasons you can't find meaning and success on your own terms, here are some practices to help you overcome those limiting beliefs.

- Write down all the reasons why you can't get what you want. Then ask yourself, "What if I could? What if there was a way to do it? Who's already doing it that I could talk to?" Or have someone else ask you the questions, because your answers are often different when someone else asks.

- Begin to notice your self-limiting beliefs as they arise in your mind and label them: "Aha, there you are ... trying to keep me from having what I want." Hear it. Notice it. And move on to a more productive thought.

- Think of someone you know who's been able to have the kind of company and life you want. Pretend to be that person. When you feel stuck, ask yourself, "What would so-and-so do now?"

- Vividly imagine yourself getting what you want. See, feel, and hear yourself in the future when you're happy and successful, living a life with meaning.

- One of my favorite new tools is quantum jumping. It starts from the principle of quantum physics that you can be in two places at the same time. You basically assume that there's a "you" out there who already has what you want, and so you jump to that state and track how you feel, what you're surrounded by, and how you operate—and then you bring those characteristics back with you.

It's crucial that you work with your self-limiting beliefs, because otherwise they'll act as brakes on your mind. They'll cause you to think too narrowly and to lower your aspirations, so that you fail to create the company and the life that is uniquely yours, and will therefore rob the world of the fullness of what you have to offer.

There's just no time to waste. The world needs each and every SheEO with a great idea we can find. Since everything is broken, we have to get on it. My friend Tom Hadfield is an honorary SheEO who created three successful businesses before he was thirty. He did his undergrad at Harvard, and because he was one of the top students, he got invited to the Goldman Sachs recruiting tour. The speaker was a thirtysomething guy who was talking on and on about what a successful leader he was and how he'd made $40 million the year before. Tom stood up and said, "Given the state of the world and all the challenges we face, how can you justify using your leadership that way?"

How are you, how am I, using our leadership, our creativity, our talents, and energy? We have a choice—let's make sure it's for something that matters. As the Escape the City manifesto says, "Life is too short to do work that doesn't matter to you."

We want to know our work has meaning.
That we're moving the needle on creating the kinds
of changes that are needed in the world.
#IamASheEO

Women tend to focus on finding meaningful
solutions to real problems.
#IamASheEO

Meaning gives you the "why"; and in order to
build a powerful "what," you need to be in touch
with your powerful "why."
#IamASheEO

Meaning carries energy: "Nothing is going to
stop me from doing this."
#IamASheEO

Autonomy + Mastery + Purpose are the intrinsic
motivators of high performance.
#IamASheEO

Take out entrepreneur insurance: a sense of
meaning can help you cope with life's challenges
and stresses.
#IamASheEO

Find your tribe—to be successful you don't
have to go it alone.
#IamASheEO

You can create your own customized version
of success—you just have to claim it.
#IamASheEO

We live in the age of total customization, yet when we
talk about success, it's a cookie-cutter template.
#IamASheEO

PRINCIPLE **3**

YOU CAN'T BE SOMEONE ELSE AND LEAD

I will not have my life narrowed down. I will not bow down to somebody else's whim or to someone else's ignorance.

—bell hooks

Holly Ruxin spent much of her career at Goldman Sachs and Morgan Stanley, where the world she lived in was all about power and money. As Holly says, "The people with the best strategy on how to make money for the company, at any cost, and often with the sharpest knives (to stab you in the back) won, every time." However, that power dynamic is now changing in every part of society. Information is out there. Transparency is increasing, and as one headline recently proclaimed, the world is becoming about relationships. We're swinging the pendulum away from the fully masculine toward the feminine, where caring relationships and humanity bring you the new power. We're moving toward a perfect dynamic mix of the masculine and the feminine, and therefore a financial company can be fantastic at what they do but also be about giving and not just about taking profits.

Holly's recognition of this transformation and her desire to change her own life led her in 2012 to launch Montcalm TCR, a wealth management firm based on extensive expertise in capital markets and an understanding of the patterns in the financial markets, paired with a foundation of integrity, love, and compassion. When Holly first started talking to colleagues about her vision for more humanity in the financial markets and in the companies that run them, they told her she was unrealistic. All people care about is making as much money as possible, she was reminded. But that was the old game. Holly's vision is about transforming that paradigm. When clients ask her what they should be investing in, she tells them it's the wrong question. "I'll worry about the investments. That's my expertise," she explains. "And I'll manage the appropriate risk/reward for your personal circumstances. What I want to know from you is, what do you really want from what you have?"

Holly focuses her clients' portfolios on investments that have sustainable and understandable returns, which reduces her clients' fears in an increasingly fragile and interconnected financial market. She then meets with the whole family and hears from everyone about what they care about. "We get to know people and we take care of them. They come back to us and refer us to their friends because we care and because we provide financial stability they can count on," says Holly. "I can't tell you the number of thank-you notes I've received from clients, something that rarely happened at my previous firms."

Holly is a wonderful example of SheEO Principle 3: you can't be someone else and lead. Despite a successful career in traditional wealth management, she left the comfort of that established world and risked being truly herself.

In our first SheEO cohort, it was Ursula Burns, the CEO of Xerox, who made the statement about having to be yourself in order to lead. She told the story about how, when she meets young women in her organization, she often asks them what they want for themselves. "I want to be you," they say. "Well," she responds, "there's only one position in this company of fifty thousand people, and that's me. So are you going to have a life of not being satisfied? Because there's a very limited pool of CEOs of major corporations. So how are you going to create and measure success for yourself?"

This is the heart of the SheEO philosophy: you need to be yourself and play your own game, to claim your authenticity, in order to create exactly what it is you have to offer the world. Being authentic means you're true to your personality, values, and way of doing things. It requires three things that M.J. writes about in her book *Trusting Yourself*:

- **Self-awareness:** This is who I am.

- **Self-acceptance:** It's good that I'm like this.

- **Self-confidence:** I can rely on what I know and do to take meaningful action in the world.

When you grow your self-awareness, self-acceptance, and self-confidence, you can't help but realize your full potential. It's an automatic upward spiral. The more self-aware and self-accepting you are, the more you can rely on yourself to make wise choices and the more your self-confidence and self-acceptance grows.

This is not to say it's easy, especially for women. That was certainly true for me. I always felt like a bit of an outsider. I played a lot of sports and did well in school, but all the while I was looking for something that would inspire me, that felt like something I could spend my life doing. I knew I had a role to play in the world, but I had no idea what it was. I didn't want to take on any of the traditional roles I saw around me. None of what my parents' friends were doing seemed like something I'd like to spend my life doing.

Then one day we went to visit my uncle, who'd lived in India and Africa. I remember standing in the kitchen where their son was eating a mango. I'd never seen a mango before; it was totally exotic to me. And their whole house was full of art and sculptures that had stories attached to them from their travels around the world. It was intoxicating: I wanted to have a life full of experiences like that. I wanted to be free to explore and travel and discover new things. There was a world out there that I was interested in, but I lacked the self-confidence and self-awareness to know how to access it. I remember wondering how I could get a "job" (at the time I never thought about creating my own thing) that would give me that experience. And what exactly did I want to be?

I talked about these worries with my uncle, and he said something that changed my life: "It's not about having the list of who you're going to be. It's about making a list of everything you think you *might* be and then striking things off after you've tried them."

It was hard to get my head around that at first. I was surrounded by a lot of people who didn't seem as confused as I was. Some of my friends knew exactly what they wanted to do, so I thought I was either wrong or incomplete. Now, of course, with hindsight I can see that in many cases they were just following what someone had told them they should want and didn't really give it another thought.

I decided to heed my uncle's advice. I thought, "Well, I'm doing really well at university and my favorite professor suggested I do my masters." So I did my masters and was thinking of becoming an academic. I applied to the PhD program, and then, in a long conversation with one of my professors one day, he complained that he didn't have control over what he really wanted to do. He didn't want to teach at all. He wanted to write. And this was a professor who was at the top of his field. So I realized that academia wasn't going to give me the freedom I was searching for.

Next up on my list of possibilities was diplomat. I was fascinated by foreign policy, and since there were so few women in the field, I thought I might be able to break ground there. Then I met a diplomat who was incredible at what he did, and I watched him in action. I soon realized that there was no way I could do his job because I'm not great at smooth-talking people, negotiating middle ground, and, well, being diplomatic. Cross that off.

I ended up trying many different things, including launching my first business, continually experimenting, and striking things off the list. It was a wonderful time of experimentation. From what worked and what didn't, I learned what I was good at, what I was passionate about, what motivated me.

Something that really helped on my search was journaling. When I was eighteen, my grandmother gave me my first journal. She also showed me her own journals—she'd written in one every day since she went off to university at eighteen. Writing to get my thoughts out of my head was very useful, I found. It created the space to express what I was feeling and work out my hopes, dreams, fears, and ambitions. For me it was an intuitive process of developing self-awareness, self-acceptance, and self-confidence, so that by the time I was thirty, I had a much better idea of who I was and a strong belief that I could do anything I wanted. For most of us, understanding who we are and what we want to do isn't something we wake up all of a sudden and know. Well, maybe it is for some people, but for me it's been a constant struggle between glorious, and painful, aha moments.

I strongly encourage you to do the work on yourself so that you can stand in your authenticity. If you don't fully embrace yourself in your uniqueness, if you follow others rather than lead, you'll end up constantly second-guessing yourself—"Am I doing this the right way?"—and that'll get in the way of being successful.

M.J. recently worked with a SheEO who was stalled precisely this way. She had an idea for a social venture that was similar to one a famous person had created. Instead of tuning in to who she was and what she truly wanted to create, she kept asking herself, "Did he did do this? Did he do that? But I can't do what he did. So maybe I can't do this." She was completely stuck because she believed she had to be him in order for her idea to succeed. M.J. helped her to stop focusing on how the other person had done it, to get in touch with her own passion and strengths, and to trust that she could do it her way. Within a month she'd gathered around her a group of people committed to the idea and quickly raised $2 million to get started.

This is not to say that you can't learn from example. There is tremendous wisdom to be had from other people's success. But it has to be pulled through the lens of your own personal vision, values, and ways of working. You can't, for instance, decide to follow the model of how Debbie Fields started and grew Mrs. Fields Cookies, because you're not Debbie and this isn't the 1970s. You can, however, read her story and think about how what she did might apply to you and your idea. But first you must truly understand and embrace yourself. The more you do, the more you'll create something unique in the world that will be attractive to others—investors, customers, and employees alike.

Don't just take my word for it. In a great article entitled "Entrepreneurs: You're More Important Than Your Business Plan," Rich Leimsider and Cheryl Dorsey, members of Echoing Green, an angel investor and grant maker in social enterprise, talk about how entrepreneurs ask them to review their business plans all the time. But what matters more to them than a good business plan, they say, is who the founders are. Particularly in bootstrapping businesses, they claim, "resilience trumps planning and energy trumps experience." That's why they look for four key characteristics in the people they fund:

- **Purpose and Passion:** Is this something they truly care about?

- **Perspective and Resilience:** Do they have the ability to overcome the obstacles they will inevitably encounter as they build their business?

- **Visionary Leadership:** Is their idea transformative, and can they rally others behind it to turn it into a reality?
- **Power Source and Resource Magnetism:** Can they attract money, people, and other resources to their cause?

The more authentic you are, the more passionate you are about your idea, and the more you're able to bounce back from setbacks, the more you'll succeed. That's because when a person is in her authenticity, we're naturally drawn to her because she's showing up in her truth. The ultimate "business" pursuit is to find your truth, because then it's easy: it's just being yourself.

MASTERY + MEANING = SUCCESS

You must lead as yourself and not follow for another important reason: we're living in a dramatically different time than ever before, with new, unchartered dynamics. Predictability is out the window. We can't count on anything that worked in the past working in the future. That doesn't mean it won't, just that we can't predict it as we used to. I think of a statistic I heard from Nortel, the now-defunct Canadian telecom company. During the craziness of the last dot-com boom, it claimed that 50 percent of its revenues came from products that weren't even on the whiteboard a year before.

That's why, when people ask me for advice and present a very rational business model that sounds like every other thing I've seen over the last twenty years, I say, "That's probably not going to work." Because everything is turning upside down. What's working is the reverse of how things have worked in the past.

The flipped classroom, popularized by the Khan Academy, is a great example. Rather than getting content in class from the teacher and then doing assigned problems at home, students learn new content by watching video lectures online, usually at home, while classroom time is spent doing "homework," with the teacher offering individualized help. It's proving so successful that many educators see it as the wave of the future for learning.

Because we're living in such a dynamically changing time, in order to be successful as SheEOs, we must be able to flip things on their head and challenge our assumptions about the way things are. This means positioning ourselves in front of the curve, being responsive and adaptive to the rapid pace of change. Take the Flip camera—enormously successful when introduced in 2006, it was a dead product by 2011 because of the introduction of video cameras into phones. In 2009, when Cisco bought in for $590 million, it obviously couldn't see what a disastrous investment it had just made. That's how fast things are changing.

Because things are so volatile and fast-moving, there's nothing that's guaranteed, no sure things, no no-brainers. Nothing that you can absolutely guarantee on the outside. But what you can absolutely count on is *you*—your passion, your resilience, your creativity. I'm working with a twentysomething SheEO right now who's on her first startup. She's all in, 100 percent committed; she hopes to grow her organization and sell it. At this point, whether the business will succeed is unclear. But she's unafraid. "Whether or not this works," she recently said to me, "I will have learned so much that I can bring to my next idea."

This is a very different notion of success than in the past. I think of it as a formula: mastery + meaning = success. When you grow your mastery and what you're doing has meaning for you, you're being successful. You learn from each experience and then move on to the next thing. And over time you'll acquire a portfolio of experience and a network of people that will allow you to create more and greater things.

We looked at meaning in the preceding chapter. Here we're focusing on the other aspect of the equation: mastery. According to the dictionary, *mastery* is defined as "the possession of consummate skill." It requires knowing who you are and what you're passionate about enough to do the work to develop that level of skill. In his book *Outliers*, Malcolm Gladwell popularized the idea that ten thousand hours of appropriately guided practice was "the magic number of greatness." What are you willing to put in that amount of time for? What have you already devoted a huge amount of time to just because you love it?

DO WHAT YOU LOVE, LOVE WHAT YOU DO

Years ago, Marsha Sinetar wrote a book called *Do What You Love and the Money Will Follow*. It's about how following your passions is the pathway to success. It makes sense, doesn't it? When you do what you love, you're willing to work hard at it, so you're more likely to be masterful and therefore more likely to succeed. You're more likely to experience flow, so you create success more effortlessly. When you do what you love, you're happy, and happiness is magnetic, so you naturally draw others who want to engage with you. When you do what you love you love to do it, so you're willing to keep at it when the going gets tough. Doing what you love generates all the characteristics that the Echoing Green investors look for in an entrepreneur: passion, resilience, leadership, and magnetism.

If the idea that you can generate more success by doing what you love sounds too pie in the sky, consider this study of fifteen hundred young people. Group A was made up of 1250 folks who chose a career for money. Group B was composed of 250 people who chose a career because it was what they loved to do. Researchers followed both groups for two decades. After twenty years, 101 were millionaires—and only one of them came from Group A. Of the 250 people who chose their passion, 100 of them became wealthy. Virtually no one who chose for money did.

The role of passion in success is often overlooked because most of us hold the erroneous belief that following our passion requires settling for less money and success. Nothing could be further from the truth. Over and over, studies of self-made millionaires show that their wealth was a byproduct of doing what they loved.

Getting in touch with your passion is critical as a SheEO, because it's your passion that will give you the drive, commitment, and energy necessary to create whatever it is you desire. It's part of the special sauce of your authenticity. If you aren't sure where your passions lie, try completing the following statements.

1. If money were no object and I was guaranteed success, I would …

2. If I could star in my own how-to TV show, it would be about …

3. I get excited when I …

4. I love to learn about and/or teach others about …

Your passion is uniquely yours. It can't be faked. It can come from some deep love you were born with or it might be forged from some challenge or hardship. Either way, passion is the engine for most great ideas.

Take Michelle Crosby. Her parents had a messy divorce when she was five. By nine, she was being asked by the court which parent she would prefer to live with. She knew by then that there had to be a better way. Her passion to make divorce better, especially for kids, led her to law school and to the creation of Wevorce, a mediation-enabling technology company that offers amicable divorce planning, co-parent planning, a parenting agreement, financial mapping, financial agreements, and divorce settlement for roughly one-third of what a traditional divorce costs. In less than a year, she's secured $1 million in funding, is operating in six states, and has been featured in *Forbes*, the BBC, *The New York Times*, *Entrepreneur* magazine, and Fox Business, among others. The media has embraced her because she's willing to tell her story about why she cares so deeply about the issue. That's leading with who you authentically are.

DIFFERENTIATION IS CRITICAL

The other reason why authenticity is so important now is that in a world of seven, soon to be nine, billion people, all connected together and all seeking ways to earn a living, you can't possibly stand out if you're a follower. And if you don't stand out, you'll get run over. Remember that, given the vast number of people on the planet, there's most likely a market for precisely what you've created as long as it's unique. Because then you'll attract those customers who want exactly what you have to offer. But if it's generic—just another cookie, for instance—you won't stand out enough from the crowd to be noticed by your potential market. When you truly embrace who you are, you'll create something that's uniquely yours, just as Michelle Crosby of Wevorce did.

Or Shamini Dhana. Shamini runs Dhana EcoKids, which offers the first organic, fair trade, sustainable apparel for kids aged four to twelve. Shamini is a former corporate manager who decided to create a company that combines her passions for fashion, nature, and helping children adopt a green philosophy. Her message is that "every action and choice we make has an impact not only on our lives, but also that of our earth. To be mindful of how powerful a thought and a behavior can be. That in order for us to live in peace and harmony with one another, we must respect Mother Nature and the gifts she has blessed us with." Dhana EcoKids was recently named one of the top three sustainable children's wear brands globally.

THE FIVE QUESTIONS

Whenever a budding entrepreneur comes to me for mentorship, I ask five questions that came from a project KidsNRG did for Xerox in the 1990s. Xerox asked us to help them with the question "What is the mission statement for the learning environment in the future?" We had a team of amazing young people digging into the question for four days. The folks from Xerox had brought in boxes full of mission statements and studies on learning. The kids looked through them and then fairly quickly tossed all the studies aside. "If this is about learning," they said, "it can't be a statement. It has to be a question. And the question is, 'What do you want?' But wait—is there really one question? It has to start with 'What do you want?' then go to 'What do you have?' and 'What do you need?' Then, 'How are you going to get it?' and then, 'What are you going do with it?'"

These young people gave a forty-five-minute presentation to Rhys Davies of Xerox, outlining the process they went through in coming up with each question. By the end, he was tremendously moved. He said, "You've just created the learning environment of the future during this project." Davies was so inspired by the questions that he put them on the back of his business card. Since then, psychologists have studied other versions of these questions, and they're now considered the unlocking questions for learning.

Taken together, these five questions will help you understand what you're aiming for, what resources you have to get there, what resources you need to develop or find, how you might go about doing that, and what you want to do with what you've created once you've achieved your goal. It's important to answer that last question because it tests the point of all your efforts. For example, if you answered the first question by saying you wanted to be president of Xerox, it's critically important to know what you're going to *do* as president of Xerox. This last question often reframes the first, because once you get clear on that, you may see that where you end up isn't what truly matters to you. Then you can go back and start with the first question again, being more real about what you want.

In fact, most people don't think that last question through. I'm part of a network at the World Economic Forum called the Global Leaders for Tomorrow (now Young Global Leaders), and every year they choose a hundred young people (under thirty-four) from around the world who show exceptional potential. They can be from government, business, academia, or NGOs. My class had the number two at a top oil company, the number three at a global restaurant chain, and the finance minister of country X. But in my experience, at least 30 percent of each class of GLTs are in transition, trying to figure out what to do now that they've reached the top of their profession in their mid-thirties. They prove that it's easy to follow the "game" and pursue the stated goal of traditional success. But is that really going to get you where you want to be?

Try the five questions for yourself and see where they take you:

1. What do you want?

2. What do you have?

3. What do you need?

4. How are you going to get it?

5. What are you going to do with it once you get it?

Let's use as an example a wonderful young entrepreneur I know, Anne-Marie Paquette, who co-founded StrokeLink, a business I was a mentor with. Sixty percent of stroke victims go home without a rehabilitation plan. If they do get something from the hospital, it's usually photocopied pencil drawings of stick figures doing exercises. If Stroke-Link can solve this problem, it may mean that far fewer people are admitted back into the hospital after having strokes, and that many more might recover quicker. Now that's something worth pursuing.

Here's how Anne-Marie responded to the five questions.

1. **What do you want?** I want to create a business that helps people who've recently regained their independence by providing access to high-quality rehabilitation resources.

2. **What do you have right now?** I have experience gained from my internships in rehabilitation centers; my co-founder has some experience; I've created a mock-up of an iPad app; and I have a technical lead, someone with business savvy, and a network of people I could reach out to for help.

3. **What do you need?** I need credible partners, a technologist, and expert advisers; I also need to figure out a business model.

4. **How are you going to get it?** I'm going to work with rehabilitation clinics, find the best, validated exercises, and develop partnerships with experts in stroke care.

5. **What are you going to do with it once you get it?** We'll increase the number of stroke victims with access to high-quality therapy resources, and build a tool that helps them communicate with their caregivers.

When we do this practice in SheEO, many women discover that their idea for their business isn't actually tied to what they really want. They've come up with a "good" business idea, but it's not going to get them what they truly desire. This is because often someone will suggest something to us, or something falls into our lap, and we just start working on it. But faced with the question of whether it's what they want, some women realize that it's not.

If you find that to be true for you, consider it a creation opportunity. How can you tie it in? How can you connect what you're doing with where you want to be? For instance, an entrepreneur told me that she wanted to create a big environmental organization and build a billion-dollar company. I challenged her: "What if they were the same thing? What if you could loop them together?"

DARE TO BE REAL

Telling yourself the truth of what you really want takes courage. Half the time when people talk to me they're stuck because they're thinking, "I need to do this." But doing it from a place of "have to" rather than "want to" is a death trap. It rarely creates success. And even if it did, what good is that to you? Unless you're completely in, what's the point?

But many of us don't even dare to ask that question because we think that what we want isn't relevant: "I have to go to work and make money, so I can't have what I want." Telling yourself the truth about what you want and believing you can have it is a muscle. I know because I've built it up over the years. I can remember the first time someone said to me, "So, what do you want?" I said, "It doesn't matter what *I* want. I'm doing client work. All I need to know is what the client wants so that I can be successful." And she said, "But what do *you* want?"

Back and forth we went. I kept saying the same thing, until finally it hit me. You can't create greatness unless you're a part of it. Even with clients, what you want is as important as what they want. It has to be win–win for both of you; otherwise, you'll only get mediocrity. You create greatness only when what you're doing is totally aligned with who you are, what you believe, and what you want to do. When you're in your integrity.

That's why this book and the SheEO program is fundamentally a self-exploration. There are scads of advice out there in every known form—books, articles, DVDs, websites, programs—on how to start and run a business. I'm interested in helping you uncover and discover the business that only *you* can create because it's the expression of your passion, your strengths, and the impact you want to have in the world.

This focus on knowing yourself deeply and being authentic as a key to business success is usually surprising to the women entering the SheEO program. Here's how Jessica Knox, SheEO of Teamwave, described her experience.

> *Over the past month I had a transformative learning experience—and "transformative" is not a term I use lightly. I'm*

building a new business, and applied to SheEO, an incubator specifically for women-led startups....

The first day we filed into the room to find a circle of pillows on the floor. "Okay, I get it, they're trying to create a 'feminine' space," I thought to myself. We sat down with our game faces on, ready to talk business—to pitch, to talk revenue streams.

What happened next shook me. The incubator founders ... told us their stories. Not a reiteration of their LinkedIn bios, but how their personal struggles and dreams shaped them and influenced their lives as entrepreneurs. The impact of their sincerity on the room was palpable.

That day we didn't talk business at all. Instead, we delved deep into who we are and what we want. Through their alarming authenticity, these women had created an instant trust that allowed me to look firmly in the mirror and start to share my reflection with the group. This is not something I've done in a business context. Ever....

Everything I learned from then on was grasped through a different lens. I constantly challenged myself with self-reflection. Was I staying true to my values and personal goals? Which of my strengths and internal barriers were affecting my outcomes? I've made leaps and bounds in evolving my business as a result.

This authentic approach flies in the face of so much of the advice out there for women entrepreneurs. A recent article in *The Boston Globe* that really got my blood boiling was written by MIT Sloan School of Management professor Fiona Murray. She was appropriately decrying the paltry number of women who get funded by VCs (7 percent). But her solutions were all about how women needed to be more like men to appeal to the fortysomething male VCs. Among her ideas? Wear a uniform, not a fussy dress that gets caught in the microphone, and watch sports so that you can bond! This is advice for businesswomen in 2014?

I'm proud to be part of a movement to transform how we think about ourselves and what we women want as entrepreneurs. Years ago, I heard Air Yaratne speak at the Alliance for the New Humanity conference. He's considered the Gandhi of Sri Lanka. "Greed is so well organized that we call it economic prosperity," he said. "Ill will is so well organized that we call it defense and we make weapons and war, and ignorance is so well organized that we study everything except ourselves." In that moment, I realized that the only thing that truly matters is understanding ourselves and why we're here, and then figuring out how to contribute what we have.

You have this one incredibly beautiful life to live. What do you want to do with it? What kind of world do you want to live in and how do you want to help create that? Imagine if life were a giant experiment to see what we can create together and individually. If you start from that creation space, you'll recognize that you have an opportunity to build something. The best way to predict the future is to create it. So what do you want to create? What kind of society serves you and serves me?

BREAKING THROUGH THE FEAR BARRIER

Amway CEO Doug DeVos was recently interviewed on the Market-Watch website about his company's latest annual study of entrepreneurship. After conducting interviews in twenty-four countries, they found that people generally believed entrepreneurs to be the engine of economic growth, and that although many wanted to start their own business, they had encountered barriers. No, it wasn't financing that topped the list of barriers, although that was, of course, mentioned. It was fear of trying something different, followed by concerns about training ("Am I prepared?"); support ("Can I find the mentors I'll need?"); making a mistake ("If I make a mistake will I get a chance again?"); and timing ("Is this the right time?"). As you can see, the majority of these barriers are internal: fear of taking a risk, fear of inadequacy, fear of not being able to find help, fear of failure. In other words, the greatest barrier to starting a business is your own mind.

What's standing in your way? What are your greatest fears about being a SheEO? Bringing them to consciousness allows you to find solutions. Afraid of taking a risk? What would make it easier—having a mentor? A partner? Starting small? What's one step you could take that would give you more confidence? Want to make sure you have support? Join a SheEO cohort, as I talk about in Principle 8. Whatever your fear is, bring it to the surface and begin to find ways to increase your comfort level. Throughout this book, you'll find inspiration, suggestions, and support for dealing with your fears and overcoming self-imposed limitations.

We all have internal barriers to stepping into our authenticity and daring to be as big as we could be. We all have those voices in our heads, those thoughts that, if we don't bring them to the surface and transform them, will ruin us: "I'd love to do this, but here are the six reasons why I'm not good enough." "I should do this, but...." I gave you some practices for overcoming limiting beliefs in Principle 2. And yet this is such a common roadblock for SheEOs that I want to offer five other ways to move beyond your self-imposed limitations.

1. BAN "SHOULDS" AND "CAN'TS"

I've practiced shedding from my lexicon words like *should* and *can't* because, as my husband likes to say, "can't" means "won't." One way to do this is to ask your partner, team, or cohort to let you know when they hear you say those limiting things so that you can become more aware of your unconscious barriers. It's way easier when you have people pointing it out to you. The more you notice them and then drop them, the less they'll run you.

2. "SCRIPT" IT

Another technique I like to use to break through my internal barriers is to recognize the pattern in my reactions, build a script around that pattern, and then have someone else read it out loud to me. When you hear it from the outside, it's surprising how crazy it sounds. And yet such scripts control us until we let them surface and then let them go.

Here's an example of one I did at the Zen Monastery Peace Center retreat with Cheri Huber in California. I was drawing and taking notes at the retreat while people were talking, because I find that it helps me focus. After our session, the facilitator left a note for me: "Would you be willing to pay full attention by putting away your paper and pencils?"

> **VOICE 1 (Intolerant):** #$%%^ you! It helps me focus.
>
> **VOICE 2 (Compassionate):** Okay. Clearly he doesn't know about different learning styles. Maybe you should explain to him that writing notes helps you focus and listen more clearly.
>
> **VOICE 1 (Intolerant):** He should already know that. What's his problem?
>
> **VOICE 3 (Victim):** I really resent the fact that he thinks I'm not being present. I *am* being present.
>
> **VOICE 4 (Fear of confrontation):** Let's just talk to Cheri when this is over and tell her that her facilitator doesn't get it.
>
> **VOICE 2 (Compassionate):** Well, what if this was a learning moment for him and he'd find it helpful?
>
> **VOICE 1 (Intolerant):** He doesn't deserve my help.

... and on and on.

As this script shows, when someone confronts me with something I don't agree with, I often go on the offensive. Then I switch to defensive, then avoidant, then compassionate, and back to offensive again. It's my pattern. And it's something I'm working on. We all have our ways of reacting to things. As Cheri says, the way we do one thing is the way we do everything, so it's important to recognize your pattern in order to be aware of it when it arises.

3. HANG THEM UP—LITERALLY

My meditation teacher, Cheri Huber, has a wonderful practice for dealing with internal barriers. It's a great way of making visible to yourself the thoughts that are cluttering up your life. When you become aware of those negative voices, first name them, and then dress them—put an outfit on a hanger and hang it up in your room with the name of that voice on the outfit—and walk by them for a few days. Taking them outside of you and seeing them hanging there makes them less powerful. Eventually you'll get to realize that they're just voices, and that you can listen to them or not. You'll get tired of them, and they'll lose their power over you.

4. MEDITATE TEN MINUTES A DAY

I've been doing mindfulness meditation since 2002. My first experience was a ten-day silent meditation retreat. It was hell to go through. I remember how painful it was to sit for twelve to fourteen hours a day and work to calm the voices in my head. But it kick-started me in a way that was remarkable. Prior to going to the retreat, if I dropped something I'd automatically say, "#$&%!" After the retreat, when I dropped something, I'd just look at the floor and think, "Oh, I dropped something." I didn't react at all. What a gift. Since then, the biggest thing that keeps me meditating is how productive and present I can be. Actually, I think meditation is the secret productivity tool of the millennia. The more grounded, clear, and non-reactive you are, the easier it is to get stuff done. Calm and clear, on demand. That's the foundation of emotional intelligence.

People have been meditating for centuries, but researchers have recently begun to understand from a scientific point of view why it's so useful. According to Daniel Siegel, clinical professor of psychiatry at the UCLA School of Medicine and executive director of the Mindsight Institute, ten minutes of mindfulness meditation a day creates mindsight, the ability of your mind to notice what it's doing. And the more you're aware of what your mind is doing, the more freedom you have to respond to things in a new, fresh way. Once you're aware of the old, limiting thought, you can choose whether you want to listen to it. But without mindsight, you're not even aware of it in the first place. Your inner voices are simply running you.

That's why cultivating mindsight is one of the best things we can possibly do for ourselves—it gives us awareness, and ultimately choice, about what we think and how we respond. If you want to get started on a mindfulness practice, see the SheEO website (www. IamaSheEO.com) for resources. Siegel's research shows that you can build the mindsight muscle in as little as ten minutes a day.

5. FORGET THE WHY

I can't tell you how many times a week I'll be in a conversation with someone about internal barriers and they ask, "But why am I like this?" Or, "Why can't I let it go?" It's so easy to get caught up in trying to figure out why we have these self-limiting beliefs. But understanding why doesn't actually help us change. As M.J. wrote in her book *This Year I Will*, understanding why is the booby prize. It may be interesting and it may be insightful, but you still have to do the work of change. And for that, you need to know what it is that's standing in your way, and how you're going to relate to it differently.

YOU *CAN* CHANGE—AND YOU CAN CHANGE THE WORLD

If, when you become aware of your internal barriers, you think, "That's just the way I am," we're learning now that this isn't the case. It's absolutely possible to transform yourself, to shift from the way you've been into something new. I remember when I first heard Deepak Chopra say, "Every single cell in your body is changing constantly, and every seven years you're a completely new person molecularly." The idea of such transformation every seven years is exciting to me because it means that I can create myself anew. So instead of saying things like "I can't do that," I say, "I can't do that yet" or "I haven't done that yet." Or, "In the past, I've been like this." It leaves open the door of possibility. Just because that's how you've been in the past doesn't mean you're stuck that way. I find that quite freeing.

I love this Marianne Williamson quote from *Return to Love*; it inspires me whenever I limit myself: "Our deepest fear is not that we are inadequate. Our deepest fear is that we are powerful beyond measure. It is our light, not our darkness that most frightens us. We ask ourselves, 'Who am I to be brilliant, gorgeous, talented, fabulous?' Actually, who are you not to be?"

You and I can change. And we do. The more we relate differently to our inner voices, the more we meditate, and the more we step back and observe how we're being in the world, the more we can course-correct on our path to be bold, to be as great as we can be, and to build the organizations, companies, and initiatives that change the world.

Being authentic means you're true to your personality,
values, and way of doing things.
#IamASheEO

Do the work on yourself so that you can
stand in your authenticity.
#IamASheEO

Learning from others has to be pulled through
the lens of your own personal vision, values, and
ways of working.
#IamASheEO

What you can absolutely count on is *you*, your passion,
your resilience, your creativity.
#IamASheEO

We can define success in new ways:
mastery + meaning = success.
#IamASheEO

Do what you love, love what you do.
#IamASheEO

You create greatness only when what you're doing
is totally aligned with who you are, what you believe,
and what you want to do.
#IamASheEO

Inside out, not outside in.
#IamASheEO

PRINCIPLE **4**

IT DOESN'T HAVE TO BE HARD

I can do everything with ease on the stage, whereas in real life I feel too big and clumsy. So I didn't choose acting. It chose me.

—Ingrid Bergman

A year ago or so, I was serving as a mentor in a program that develops young entrepreneurs. Selection weekend is particularly challenging, as it's down to the top seventy-two most entrepreneurial students in the country and only thirty-six get selected. The young people are grilled with questions that can often unground them. For example, when one of the young women was asked about her business idea, she talked about making whoopee pies and selling them across campus. But as she told her story, there was something about her that wasn't really coming out, so they probed deeper: "What interests you? Tell us more." It turned out that she actually had another idea—a whole new way of tracking deficiencies on construction sites. She'd noticed that people at these sites were still tracking construction problems by making notes on a clipboard, which then had to be written up as a report back at the office. Her idea was an app that enabled construction workers to take a picture and send it to the contractor via email—everything trackable with one click.

It was a fabulous idea, but she hadn't led with it because it felt so obvious to her that she'd dismissed its value. In fact, she was so focused on the whoopee pie business, all the while sitting on a golden business idea, that she almost didn't get accepted into the program.

Fortunately, after sharing that insight, she got in. And within six months she was piloting the app with major contractors in Canada and was well on her way to a burgeoning business.

Pretty incredible story, right? But to the SheEO way of thinking, it's actually not exceptional. That's what Principle 4 is about—building your business doesn't have to be hard. You can do it with ease. It takes effort, of course, but it's what I'd call easeful effort. Unfortunately, until we truly embrace this notion, we often miss the easy or effortless insights, looking for something hard.

That's because this principle goes against hundreds of years of beliefs about work. In the old model, we achieve success through working hard, through sacrificing our family and social life, through doing things we dislike. If you achieve something that was really hard, then it must be worthwhile. Because you had to slog and struggle through, because getting it was difficult, it had greater value.

The hardship mindset starts in school, where you're taught to jump through whatever hoops you're given. You have to work hard to get into college, then to work hard for the marks that will get you a good job, then to work hard to climb the corporate ladder. And the harder you work, the more successful you'll be. It's a belief system that has led to a huge increase in overwork, with one-third of North Americans now classifying themselves as workaholics.

These ideas about hard work originate from the Industrial Revolution and Protestant religious beliefs, which viewed hard work as a virtue and the secret to success. But they're simply not true. According to a 2010 Center on Budget and Policy Priorities report, in the last thirty years, North Americans have been working an average 20 percent more and taking less vacation. But during the same period, in the United States the gap between the wealthiest and the middle and working class has more than tripled. We're all working harder, yet we're less well off financially. Does that make sense? It's time to revise our thinking.

What if it doesn't have to be hard? What if you can create success with ease? Just look at the community connected to the four-hour work week. This emerging movement is based on working from your expertise within networks of other people—which allows everyone to contribute skills that for them are almost effortless. A great example of this is TopCoder, a network of over 500,000 technical specialists who each contribute what they're great at in order to solve big challenges for companies.

Despite such evidence, we still tend to discount things that are easy and overvalue things that are hard. M.J. likes to tell the story of her search for meaningful work in her twenties: "I'd fallen into being an editor of a weekly newspaper. I really enjoyed it. But I thought I had to find a 'career,' and was miserable because I couldn't figure it out. Then one day in my therapist's office, after I bemoaned not wanting to become a lawyer or doctor or teacher, my therapist asked me what was wrong with editing. 'It's too easy,' I said. 'Just because it's easy doesn't mean you shouldn't do it,' she replied. Finally the light bulb went off. I went on to found a book publishing company and work happily as an editor for the next twenty-five years."

We all seem to be wired to undervalue what's easy for us, and so we get stuck in this other way of working, which is really hard. And yet what's easy holds the key to our greatest success. It's the very fact that it's effortless, that you don't even have to think about it, that indicates where you can achieve the most and be the best.

WORK FROM STRENGTHS

For forty years, the Gallup Organization has conducted research on hundreds of thousands of employees on what makes individuals, teams, and companies great. Part of what it's discovered are twelve questions whose yes answers differentiate high-performing teams and individuals from average or subpar ones. One of those questions, as I talked about in Principle 2, has to do with being aligned with the mission of the organization. But the question whose answer in the affirmative revealed the greatest correlation to success was this: "At work, do you have the opportunity to do what you do best every day?" Teams that "highly agreed" were found to be 38 percent more likely to be productive and 44 percent more likely to have higher customer satisfaction scores than those that didn't.

I got excited when I first learned about this research finding, because it goes to the heart of my maxim that "it doesn't have to be hard." Gallup's studies show that when you're doing what comes naturally, you do it better and faster than others, hence creating greater productivity. Conversely, when you're doing what's difficult for you, you do it more slowly, make more mistakes, and burn out more quickly. In other words, working from strengths creates excellence, while working from weaknesses creates mediocrity. As I like to say, when you work from your greatness, greatness occurs.

According to Gallup, strengths are made up of three key ingredients: talent, knowledge, and experience. Talent is an innate way of thinking or behaving from which you operate consistently. Knowledge is the sum total of what you know about using your talent in any given situation. And experience is the amount of time you've invested in developing that talent. The more you understand, develop, and use your strengths, the more you create excellence.

There are several ways to identify your strengths. Here are the four telltale signs, according to Marcus Buckingham, author of *Go Put Your Strengths to Work*. As you read them, consider what you do and think that meet these criteria.

1. Success

- I have been very successful in this activity.
- Other people say I do this exceptionally well.
- I have rewards or recognition for doing this.

2. Instinct

- I like to do this activity every day.
- I find myself volunteering to do this often.
- This activity I perform by gut reaction.

3. Growth

- I learn how to do this very rapidly.
- I find myself thinking about this every day.
- I can't wait to learn how to do this better.

4. Needs

- I always look forward to being able to do this.

- I consider this fun, not work.

- I derive personal satisfaction from doing this.

If you want to do an in-depth exploration of your particular strengths, I especially recommend the Thinking Talent cards, map, and booklet created by Professional Thinking Partners at http://ptpinc.org/ptp-store/category/12-intellectual-diversity-products.

One easy way to know where your strengths lie is the positive feedback you get when you're doing what you're great at. Because when you produce effortless excellence, other people notice. So when you're not getting a lot of positive feedback or reinforcement, you're probably not in the right zone for you. If someone is continually criticizing your work, it's probably because you're not doing what you're great at. It's clear when you're not in your mastery, because then the work is hard. It sucks the energy out of you and you don't get good results. I consider that awesome feedback. It helps you understand where your greatness lies—and where it doesn't. That's why I don't think I've ever really fired anyone. I've just coached them out: "Hey, how's it going for you?" "Actually it's pretty crappy." "So what's that about? It seems like you're working in a space that isn't what you're great at. How do we get you into working on something that you *are* really great at?"

In the old mindset, if you're struggling, if you aren't getting great results with ease, then you need to put in more elbow grease. Spend more time, exert more effort shoring up your weaknesses. But, ultimately, you can't win at that game. In a world of soon-to-be nine billion people, you can't afford to be spending your time doing anything but being your best so that you can stand out through the excellence you create. Knowing your strengths and leveraging them to the max—that's the secret sauce of greatness with ease.

For SheEOs, the implications of this strengths research are huge. First, you should maximize the opportunities to work from your strengths every day in order to optimize success. This applies to everything from what business you create (it should allow you to predominantly use your strengths) to what kind of people you hire and/or partner with (their strengths should complement yours).

Second, if you're working solo and you don't do certain things well, you'll want to barter, trade, or pay for those things as soon as possible.

You'll never do them as well as someone else, so outsource them and put your energies on the aspects of the business you excel at. Now of course, as an entrepreneur, there are skills you must have. You have to understand financials and be able to read a spreadsheet. But are you passionate about creating the ultimate spreadsheet? I'm not, but my partner is. She's totally energized by such work every day. So rather than my doing it, I do better by partnering with her because she creates greatness in that area.

Stop focusing on shoring up your weaknesses, telling yourself and others that you "*should* be good at this." Remember, anything that has a "should" in it is dangerous. Clear the "shoulds" out of your lexicon. Consider the standard performance evaluation. Does this sound familiar? "Vicki, you're great at coming up with the big idea and getting others on board. Well done. But you're not so great at details and following through to the end. So you really should focus on tying up all the bows." What? Why in the world would you ask anyone to spend more time working on something they aren't masterful at? Who wants a company full of people spending time on their weaknesses? In my company I say, "Richard, you're masterful at coaching people, but please, please don't spend a second trying to organize an event. That's what Matt is great at. Ask him for help when something like that is on your plate!"

So if you're going to build a great company and a great team, you need to help everyone stay in their zone of strength and partner on the things they're not good at. And to do that, I've found that you have to embrace your weaknesses as well as your strengths: that way you'll know where you need help. Don't feel bad about what you can't do. Own it so that you have no trouble asking for the help you need.

WHY YOU? WHY NOW?

Ease is also a sign that you're the perfect person for your business idea and thus will be more likely to attract funding. I was reminded of this the other day while working with a bunch of super-smart guys at a startup. They were trying to figure out an idea to work on for their business and were saying things like "Let's pick something really, really hard." I asked, "Why?" "Well," one explained, "because then it would be worth it." "Really?" I replied. "What if it was really easy and you were the perfect people to do it?"

Why you? Why now? These are two of the big questions investors ask when you go to get funded. If you're seeking the hardest thing as opposed to what comes naturally, you're not likely to create uniqueness and therefore greatness. Don't be like the young woman at the start of this chapter—who almost missed the chance to create a successful product because she discounted what she knew.

Just as she does, you have something special to bring into this world. It comes from who you are and what you're great at. *That's* the business you want to build—the one that only *you* can do because it's a blend of your passions, your experience, and the issues that deeply matter to you. When you're in it all the way, it's much more likely to be differentiated because there's only one you!

Ease is a signal that this particular project or product is yours to do. Here's what I mean. When a project comes together quickly, when the stars seem to align for the idea or the partnership, I take it as a sign that it's mine to do. Conversely, when it's really hard and it's not coming together, it means that I should maybe let it go. Perhaps the timing isn't right. Or it's a great idea but not for me. Or it's the wrong combination of people. Whenever I feel I'm pushing water uphill, I need to stop and ask whether it's the right thing for me.

This doesn't mean that at the first sign of business difficulty you should bail—we all know great business stories about people who persevered and found success at the eleventh hour. The founder of Fast Company, for instance, had maxed out his credit card and was on his very last attempt to get funding when he found his angel. It's just that when it's hard, it's important to at least wonder if it's a sign that it's not right for you at this time.

Here's an example of easeful effort. In 2012, three MIT undergraduate students, including Heidi Baumgartner (Physics '14), discovered a joint passion in the Tesla coil. Their hobby project evolved into creating Tesla coil kits that they sold on eBay to DIY hobbyists. Heidi then spent her second year writing a DIY user manual for the kit and enrolled in an entrepreneurship class, where for the first time other folks referred to what they were doing as a startup. This, Heidi later explained, "surprised me because I'd considered it very much a side project that wouldn't get anywhere. I realized then that it could be bigger than my team had envisioned." The three undergrads then decided to use

Kickstarter, with a $20,000 fundraising goal, to test whether there was a market demand and to subsequently source the capital for further prototyping and a first production run. The kit found its niche, raising $169,155 (in a combination of donations and prepayment for more than five hundred preorders). The team is still in school, but the capital they accessed allowed them to hire seven employees to assemble and fulfill orders. They've now opened their own online retail store and are busy helping their "accidental" company grow.

EVERYTHING WITH EASE

I discovered working with ease the hard way. I used to believe that life as an entrepreneur had to be hard. That's what everyone said: it's 24/7, relentless, an uphill battle, et cetera. So I put out the intention to make X amount of money and to work with clients who had credibility. It *was* really hard. I was pursuing something that hadn't been done before, so there wasn't really a model to follow. And I kept trying to play someone else's game. I also started to notice that sometimes I hardly put in any effort at all and things happened, but that at other times I worked my butt off and wasn't getting results. Clearly, something wasn't working.

I sat down and thought, "What do I really want? What do I know to be true about what motivates me, what's worked before and what hasn't?" And I realized that I wanted to make X amount of money working on things that I'm great at, *with ease*. So I tried an experiment. I began to add "with ease" to my intention and was amazed at how things shifted. Soon I was hired to identify what was happening with funding women entrepreneurs around the world. I wasn't the expert in this space, but I do have a big network, so I reached out to the people I know who are portals to other people. My good friend George Petty introduced me to Suzanne Beigel, former CEO of Investors Circle in the United States, and presto, it was like hitting the jackpot. Suzanne connected me to others like her around the world, and in short order I'd put together a great list of key players and stakeholders as well as a list of gaps and opportunities. This one project has led me to a growing ecosystem of individuals and organizations who want to change the funding game for women, a key piece of the whole SheEO framework.

Now, ease and strengths are the lenses through which I look at everything: "Am I the right person to do this—can I do it with ease? Am I great at it?" But what if it's something you *have* to do that doesn't play to your strengths? Because of course we all have to do things outside our wheelhouse, at least sometimes. In those cases I ask myself, "If I have to do this, how can I do it with ease?"

Here's a recent example. I had a new startup and needed to get clients. I'm great if someone puts a person in front of me and says, "Talk to them about what we're doing." I can interest them most times. But finding the person and setting up the meeting doesn't energize me at all. To help with business development, I know I *should* be sending out an email to my network telling them what to do. I hear the "should" in my speech and realize it's an outside voice, but still, I need to get this done. I start to throw up obstacles—my contact list is a mess, I don't even know where to begin, and I just want to give up…. The "shoulds" are weighing me down with guilt and I get myself stuck.

Then I think, "How can I make this easy? I love to fix things. What if my solution solved several problems at the same time? What if it was fun, like a game?" Suddenly an idea pops in—Alphabet Business Development. "What if I start with my contacts whose names begin with A, and send out a note to one letter a day? I have about fifty A's. That'll be fifty personalized emails sent out, and I'll clean up the A's in my contact list at the same time. And what if my teammate did it, too?" Now not only have I figured out how to make it easy, but I have someone to be accountable to.

So that's what I did. Over the next month, all my contacts got cleaned up while I reached out to all these people I hadn't connected to in a while. I created customized pitches about what I was doing and found out what they were doing. And all of a sudden the task was flowing again with ease, engaging me and engaging others.

How can you make this work for you? The trick is to really understand how you tick and what motivates you. Then look at how you might use what you know about yourself to deal with what feels hard. Here's another example. M.J. is absolutely terrible at networking and marketing herself directly. She always says she couldn't sell Girl Scout cookies to her own mother. The few times she tried networking, it was a disaster. So rather than trying to get better at selling, she gets her clients with ease through the books she writes, through referrals from her relationships with satisfied clients, and by partnering with others who are good at business development. She never "sells" directly.

Working with ease means that not only do you create great results and stand out from the crowd, but you also move faster because you experience less friction. Especially when you know how to partner with others or outsource those aspects of your business that you're not excellent at, your company will succeed at an accelerated rate because you're maximizing its potential.

When you don't work from strength and ease, you create a drag—more problems pop up that take your time, energy, and focus. I'm thinking of a SheEO I know who's a wonderful visionary leader but not a good manager of people. Rather than recognize that early on, she's ended up embroiled in all sorts of personnel problems, which has distracted her from getting the investors she needs and considerably shortened her financial runway. She's in danger of going out of business, and not because her idea isn't great—it is—or because she couldn't secure funding—she did—but because she didn't follow this principle and find someone else to manage her team.

INSTANT NETWORKING

I don't like networking. I hate big rooms and crowded spaces. But when I tell people this, they have trouble believing me because I have a large network. So how did it happen? By applying the ease principle. I don't try to connect with a lot of people. Instead, when I meet one person with whom I have an instant connection, I ask them to connect me to five other people like them whom I don't already know. Why do I do that? Because when I meet someone who gets me and what I'm talking about, I know they can be a portal to other people with similar values and vision. And when you're a bit of an outlier like I am, finding people with similar values is like searching for a needle in a haystack. By leveraging people I connect with instantly, I now have a huge network of like-minded people who are interested in supporting what each of us is doing.

Have you ever met someone and felt an immediate connection? So why would you ever want it to be any different? I remember reading an article that said it takes a long time to build quality relationships, and thinking to myself, "No it doesn't." I've had mind-blowing connections with people I've only just met. Those encounters are energizing and exciting and beautiful. I always walk away with a smile on my face. So why would I "work" to build a relationship with someone when it doesn't come easily? I'm looking for my tribe. The people who get me. The people who really want to work with me. I'm not interested in convincing anyone about anything. If my message or my product or my service resonates, great. If not, there's another customer or friend or fan around the corner. Take your optimum case and make it your new bar for network building.

That's what I do with everything. Once I know something is possible in a way that's easier than what I've done before, I don't view it as an anomaly. I make it my new norm.

FINDING FLOW

Another word for ease is *flow*. Flow is that experience of being in the zone, on fire, channeling, on your game, on a roll … whatever phrase you use to describe that experience when what you're doing is completely effortless. Flow is a mental state, says psychologist Mihaly Csikszentmihalyi, in which you're "completely involved in an activity for its own sake. The ego falls away. Time flies. Every action, movement, and thought follows inevitably from the previous one, like playing jazz. Your whole being is involved, and you're using your [strengths] to the utmost."

Csikszentmihalyi, who's researched flow for decades, has identified ten factors that accompany the sense of flow, although, he says, it's not necessary to experience *all* of them for flow to occur.

1. Clear goals that, while challenging, are still attainable.

2. Strong concentration and focused attention.

3. The activity is intrinsically rewarding.

4. Feelings of serenity; a loss of feelings of self-consciousness.

5. Timelessness; a distorted sense of time; feeling so focused on the present that you lose track of time passing.

6. Immediate feedback.

7. Knowing that the task is doable; there's a balance between skill level and the challenge.

8. Feelings of personal control over the situation and the outcome.

9. Lack of awareness of physical needs.

10. Complete focus on the activity itself.

As you can see from this list, what creates flow for one person may be completely different from what creates it for someone else. The goal has to matter to you, and the activity has to be engrossing and call upon your unique talents and skills. For one person it could be writing marketing copy, for another it could be standing on stage giving a talk. Only you can find flow for yourself. The keys are having a specific goal, being challenged just the right amount, and having the outcome be dependent on your individual performance.... Sounds like the life of an entrepreneur to me!

I believe that finding flow is important for SheEOs for several reasons. First, research has shown that when we're in flow, we experience peak performance. Our brains are focused totally on the task at hand. We're in the zone of both motivation and engagement. Positive psychologists say that flow also enhances our ability to be creative and to experience less stress.

Second, flow leads to further learning and high performance. By its nature, flow requires that we be masterful at the task and feel challenged at the same time. In order to continue to experience flow, we must search out new challenges to pit ourselves against. So flow encourages us to keep getting better at what we're already good at.

Third, flow feels fabulous. Some people describe it as a deep sense of joy or rightness—the feeling that you're doing exactly what you're meant to be doing at this moment. Other people say that all emotion drops away and you're one with the doing. Whatever words you put on the experience, it's a positive one. If you were to have your brain chemistry measured during flow, writes Daniel Goleman, you'd probably have higher levels of mood- and performance-enhancing brain chemicals like dopamine. Needless to say, we're happier when we're in flow than when we're slogging.

I think there's another reason for SheEOs to track flow. It's important information about what you're meant to contribute to the world. In his book *Authentic Happiness*, Martin Seligman says something similar: that one of the characteristics of flow is the absence of consciousness—you're just doing, not thinking about doing it or judging yourself for it. And that, he speculates, should be our natural state.

Where do you find flow? What are you doing when time disappears? Studies show, no surprise, that the more a challenge requires you to use your strengths, the more likely you are to experience flow. And there's another way that matches the SheEO principles: doing work you're passionate about and that has meaning for you also tends to create flow. I hope that, in the process of reading and working with this book, you've figured out your secret formula for flow. Now it's time to put it into action!

I support creating success with ease.
Because it doesn't have to be hard.
#IamASheEO

Working from strengths creates excellence, while
working from weaknesses creates mediocrity.
#IamASheEO

When you work from your greatness, greatness occurs.
#IamASheEO

I'm committed to working with ease.
#IamASheEO

Find your flow—it encourages us to get better
at what we're already good at.
#IamASheEO,

Flow requires that we be masterful at the task
and feel challenged at the same time.
#IamASheEO

Another important reason to find your flow
is that flow feels fabulous.
#IamASheEO

PRINCIPLE **5**

YOU CAN HAVE WHAT YOU WANT

If you obey all the rules, you miss all the fun.
—Katharine Hepburn

I once got a call from a woman who was running a program for social entrepreneurship in rural Canada. She was experiencing what she perceived as a serious problem: "People are setting up centers to do social innovation, but they're all based in Toronto. The companies who want access to students for mentorships are all based there too, so we're at a disadvantage."

Here was my response: "It's perfect that you aren't in Toronto. Since we're moving to a virtual world, you can be at the forefront of creating online mentorships where mentors and mentees don't have to go anywhere to interact." What she viewed as a barrier, I saw as a huge opportunity.

This awareness is the essence of SheEO Principle 5: you can have what you want. That's my firm belief. In every situation, no matter what's going on, I assume that I can get what I want, even if I haven't figured out the how of it yet. What may seem like a barrier is simply a signal to become more creative. Rather than tell myself, for instance, that "this is the startup phase so I'll have to write proposals until we're successful enough that I can hire someone else to do it," I assume that I can get someone else to write them even though I can't yet pay or that I'll find a way around it—to work with clients who don't need to see proposals, for example. Instead of compromising on what you want, the key is to truly, absolutely believe that you can have what you want and then use possibility thinking to find a creative solution. I think of it as a stream finding its way around a rock. If you don't allow yourself to get stopped by the "rules," there are many paths forward.

The first time I saw someone "break" the rules, it blew my mind. I'd always been a rule and authority follower—whenever I came up against a limitation, I'd mostly accept it as true and move on. If someone in power said it had to be a certain way, I'd accept that without question.

But then I met Petr. I was living in Prague then and had launched a clothing business. It was just after the Wall came down, so although the Communist era was over, there was still a lot of bureaucracy. This one day, he and I were walking down a long, dark hallway in a bank. We needed to get money transferred to India in order to get a shipment of clothes sent to us, and we needed it to happen that day. The Kafkaesque hallway was full of closed doors bearing signs with the dates and times each office was open. Finally we came to the office we needed. The sign on the door said the department was open Tuesdays from one till three. This was Wednesday—and if I didn't get the funds by the end of the week, I'd be out of business.

Without a word, Petr opened the door and walked in. I followed behind, shocked. I thought to myself, "What are you doing? It's not office hours!" The bureaucrat behind the desk looked even more shocked than I was—clearly no one had ever opened the door outside of office hours before. But right away Petr distracted her by saying, "Oh, what a beautiful picture you have on your wall!" He engaged her in a conversation—"Who are the people in the picture?"—and eventually charmed her into helping us get the money.

That was the moment I realized that just because something says X doesn't mean it has to be that way. I saw that it's possible to overcome apparently insurmountable obstacles by using your creativity and innovative thinking, as Petr did, to find a way to get what you want.

This is a lesson I've learned over and over. I'm pretty accepting of the way things are until I see someone challenge an assumption or push the boundaries. Then I'm like a dog with a bone—the second I realize something is possible a different way, I make it my new normal, shedding my past thoughts and setting the bar at a new level.

It's been many years since then, and I've continued to work on removing the limits in my thinking that interfere with creating what

I want in the world. It's been a long journey. First I had to become aware of my limited thinking and then learn to ask myself a bunch of questions to challenge my assumptions and find other options. Now such thinking is automatic on my part. As soon as someone says, "I can't do this" or "This isn't possible," I say, "What if it *was* possible?" or "What's another way to get this done?"

I consider this possibility thinking a crucial skill for all SheEOs. It keeps expanding your ability to come up with new, innovative ways around the obstacles you inevitably encounter and keeps you focusing on how else you can get where you want to go. It creates persistence, one of the keys to entrepreneurial success—not in the sense of slamming your head against a wall over and over until the wall breaks down but rather in finding new ways to go over, under, or around so that the wall just crumbles before your eyes.

I think part of what's built my creative-thinking muscle is the fact that I've never had too much money to put into a project, so I've had to work around a lot of constraints. If you have a lot of financial resources to put into your business, you don't generally have to do that. You just pay someone to do what's needed. But if you don't have a big bank balance, you can really cultivate your ability to find alternative ways to solve things.

FLIPPING IT

When I face a roadblock, I dissolve it by ignoring that it's a problem. I call the technique "flipping it." You think you're up against a limitation, but then you flip it and realize that it's actually not there. For instance, you think you need $1 million to get started, and you don't have it. So what would you do if you didn't believe that thought? Where would you start? Suddenly ideas flow as to how else you can get what you want.

I always do flipping through questions, because questions engage the brain's creativity: "How can we get a shipment even though they require payment up front? How can I get help creating a website even though I can't pay?" With flipping, you have an outcome you're trying to reach, and you intend to get there despite any obstacles in your path.

Here are some examples of common obstacles and questions I use to flip them:

It's too hard.	What if it wasn't hard?
It's going to take too long.	What if you could do it faster?
I don't have enough time.	What if time is simply an excuse?
I don't have enough money.	What if you could do it with limited resources?
They just don't get it.	What do you need to do differently so that people understand you?
I really don't want to do this task.	How could you make it fun or interesting? Or do you know someone else who'd like to do it?

For each perceived obstacle, the question is designed to open your mind and increase your possibility thinking. It works whether the obstacles are in your own mind or coming from another person.

When I encounter obstacles from other people, I often have conversations like this: "I need X." "Yeah, but we don't do it that way." "Well, what if you did?" "Well, we don't." Then I switch to "How could you help me get this?" "Well, I can't because of these rules." "Okay, but is there another way?" "Well, no, there's not another way. This is how we do it." "Well, have you ever done it a different way?" "Well, maybe—" Often by asking questions and engaging the other person, together we find a way through. It's a matter of warming the person up to what it is you need and then partnering with them on a solution. I ask for advice—"How could you help me get what I want?" "If you were me, what would you do?"—to move beyond their limited thinking to a range of possible solutions. This, of course, requires some charisma. When I'm in a situation where I need to get someone on my side, I imagine myself filling up with sunshine and a giant smile, because if you're pushy it won't work.

Here are two other questions that can help you get into the flipping-it frame of mind. They're good when things look particularly problematic.

1. How can I turn this situation to my advantage?

2. What opportunities has this difficulty created that I could take advantage of?

This last question is a classic entrepreneurial one, because successful businesses can always be created from difficult situations—just as when I suggested a virtual mentorship program to the woman in the country at the beginning of the chapter.

Mallika Dutt is an example of a SheEO who's a genius at flipping it. After working in the global human rights movement for most of her professional life, she became frustrated at seeing the same faces at every conference, with the same tired policy statements that produced little or no change in the world. So she founded Breakthrough, an organization that creates provocative, uplifting media campaigns that have engaged millions of men and women in challenging deeply entrenched norms and attitudes.

One of her most innovative campaigns is called Bell Bajao (Ring the Bell), which engages men in bringing domestic violence to a halt. In the media spots, a man hears another man abusing a woman and goes and rings the doorbell to distract the perpetrator. He doesn't confront him directly, but by his presence he shows that others are watching. Bell Bajao was the first time a media campaign focused on the perpetrator instead of the victim, and Mallika took a lot of flak for partnering with men to stop their violence against women. However, her willingness to flip it created truly breakthrough results. The campaign began in India, where over 130 million people have viewed it. Surveys have shown that it's had a significant effect on changing attitudes toward domestic violence. The campaign then went global (you can check it out at www.bellbajao.org), and Mallika is working on getting one million promises from men and boys to take personal, concrete actions to end violence against women, such as supporting legislation or bringing sexual harassment policies into the workplace.

Jane McGonigal is another great flipper. She wrote a book called *Reality Is Broken*, and as the founder of Gameful, she's on a mission to create video games that solve real-world challenges. She believes in the power of games and gamers to do good in the world. According to McGonigal, the average American will have spent ten thousand hours gaming before they're twenty-one. "Video games consistently provide the exhilarating rewards, stimulating challenges, and epic victories that are so often lacking in the real world," she notes. She believes that gamers are expert problem solvers and collaborators because they regularly cooperate with other players to overcome daunting challenges. She's created games like World Without Oil, a simulation designed to avert the crisis of a worldwide oil shortage, and Evoke, a game commissioned by the World Bank Institute that sends players on missions to address issues from poverty to climate change.

Great SheEOs like Mallika and Jane know how to take advantage of the obstacle itself by flipping it to become the solution.

THE FORMULA FOR GETTING WHAT YOU WANT

For decades I'd been developing this technique of flipping obstacles and going beyond limitations in order to get what I want as an entrepreneur. Then I learned about Robert Fritz, an organizational consultant whose work focuses on how people can create what they want in the world using the laws of physics. His model confirms the SheEO principle I'm expressing here. My one-line translation of Fritz's model: put out an audacious vision and then bootstrap your way to it, making it up as you go along based on the feedback you're getting on what you're putting out there. Let's break it down so that you can try it for yourself.

Step One: Fritz says that in order to bring something new into being, you have to first tell yourself the truth about what you really want. He calls this your desired result. The criteria he thinks are important for a good desired result are these: it describes what you want to create without worrying about any possible obstacles; it comes from your passion, vision, and desire; it's positive and specific; and it focuses on the end result, not how you're going to achieve it.

Right now, take some time to articulate the result you really want. Here are examples of effective desired results from SheEOs who've gone through the program.

- Adaptive Designers builds products that transform the lives of the visually impaired.

- Sprout Guerrilla greens the world's urban centers, one blank wall at a time.

- Teamwave dramatically increases productivity in the workplace through our brain health platform.

Step Two: Once you've established your desired result, tell yourself the truth about current reality as it relates to what you want to bring into being. This allows you to see your range of potential resources as well as your potential obstacles (which you'll later flip). An effective look at current reality describes your current circumstances factually without making things better or worse than they really are or analyzing how it got to be that way.

Here's how a recent SheEO described her current reality.

> *Sprout Guerrilla ran a crowdfunding campaign and raised over $10,000 for our moss graffiti kits. The goal was $50,000, so the number fell short of where we wanted to land. When we talk to people about our product, they love the idea of having green billboards and greener spaces filled with moss graffiti. We generated a lot of media attention, interest, and excitement from people, but we didn't convert people into buyers to the degree we'd hoped. We've been targeting both businesses and individuals, which makes our messaging quite diverse. We have limited financial and human resources right now and need to find the right focus that will set us on a path for growth.*

Step Three: When you do the first two steps, it becomes clear that there's a gap between where you are and where you want to be. Fritz says this often intimidates people, but it shouldn't because the gap is actually the tension for creation. According to the laws of physics, energy wants to resolve this tension, and so moves from a less stable state to a more stable state by traveling along the path of least resistance. And the more stable state, explains Fritz, is what you want, not current reality. Current reality is always changing, but if you really want to create something, you want it today and tomorrow and out into the future. Your wanting doesn't change.

So, trusting in the process, step three is to create some actions that you think might get you closer to what you want, all the while looking for the path of least resistance. This is why you shouldn't get too caught up in "how" you'll get what you want. Until you move into action, you won't know where the path of least resistance will lead. Rather, you'll take a guess, get going, keep your eyes open for where the energy wants to go, and flip obstacles as you progress.

Here's an example: When I originally thought of SheEO as an organization, the most natural structure for it was a nonprofit. But I didn't want the world to perceive the building up of a generation of entrepreneurs as a charitable endeavor; I wanted it to perceive its value. And as I talked to people in my network, I found a lot of support for doing things a new way: SheEO could be a for-profit model for impact investing, where people would invest money expecting a social and financial return. I tried out the concept with key stakeholders and was very pleasantly surprised by their response. If I'd stuck stubbornly to what seemed the obvious nonprofit route, my mental model of how the organization "should" be funded might have precluded the alternative model that unveiled itself with ease.

This flexibility is important, says Fritz, because we can sabotage the process in three ways, all of which will be relevant to you as you bring your company into being.

1. You don't really believe you can have what you want, so you get comfortable in the gap between where you are and what you want. Then the energy for creation doesn't get activated. This is why it's crucial to nip that self-limiting belief in the bud. You *can* have it and you *will* have it, even though you don't yet know all the whens and hows.

2. Rather than motivating yourself positively by going toward what you want, you motivate yourself negatively: "If I don't do this, no one will love me; I'll be a failure." This is a process for *positive* creation. It doesn't work if you're running away rather than toward something. You have to be doing it because you really want to, not because you're afraid of what will happen if you don't.

3. You're so sure you know how it's going to happen that you use willpower alone instead of looking for the path of least

resistance. Yes, you need to push and flip limitations, but you also need to be looking for what's working and follow that.

To do this well, you have to be clear about and committed to your big concept and not give up on it no matter what—*without getting too hung up on the details*. What's important to me about SheEO is that it supports women entrepreneurs doing meaningful work and redefining winning on their own terms. That's the heart of it; it's what I'll never compromise on. How SheEO is structured organizationally, who it attracts to work with me on it—these are specifics that will emerge as it forms up over time.

Once you put your idea out there and begin to see what's coming at you, make sure you aren't creating artificial limitations to success by being too narrow in your vision or too sure about how it has to happen. It may be that what you're trying to bring into existence needs to find a different form. For instance, imagine that you want to create a website that links seniors with resources to help them live at home longer. But you keep encountering obstacles with the website. At the same time, many older people have asked you to provide them with personal recommendations instead because they don't use computers. Dig deeper. What exactly do you want? Is it a website per se? Or is it a service that helps seniors stay at home longer?

The bottom line is that you need to be paying attention to the energy that's actually coming toward you rather than your notion of what *should* be coming along. A few years ago, I told Richard that I wanted to learn about meditation. That very week, I got an invitation for a ten-day silent meditation retreat. I could have told myself that I didn't have time for it, that I was thinking about a ten-minute thing, not a ten-day one. But the minute I'd said something about meditation, this ten-day retreat is what showed up. So I acted on it, because the more I pay attention to and act on what shows up, the more things open up for me.

Here's a recent example from M.J., involving one of her coaching clients: "A woman was deeply unhappy at work. I listened to her complain for what felt like hours. One day I asked, 'If you could do anything, what would you do?' She replied, 'I'd leave my job and launch my own consulting business—I have an idea of how it could be done in a new way. But I can't do that because I could never get clients....' She proceeded to tell me all the ways it couldn't work until I interrupted, asked her to suspend her self-limiting beliefs, and taught her the Fritz process. In describing current reality, she realized she was terrible at networking, but that she was great at partnership and had a few friends who were doing similar work. In less than a month, she called to say she'd just been made a partner at one of her friend's firms. In her case, she had to let go of the idea of being a sole entrepreneur in order to achieve what she truly wanted—to be the co-owner of a venture that's changing the way consulting services are delivered with a viable client stream."

EMBRACING BOLDNESS AND RISK TAKING

It takes boldness to assume you can have what you want. But I've learned that the more I assume that, the more I get it—and the more I build my reputation as someone who thinks and acts outside the box, which in my career is a key differentiator that brings me even more opportunities.

Here's what might seem like an outrageous example. A woman emailed me from a university saying that she was holding a two-day conference and wanted to hire me to design the days. The email said, "I need six sessions with at least three speakers for each session. I want it to be really engaging." I wrote back saying, "Here's what I hear the deliverables are and yes, I'll do it under the following conditions: if I don't have to talk to you, if I don't have to be in meetings with anyone, if I can send you my thoughts in a draft by X, then you give me feedback by Y, and I iterate the final version, once, and you pay me X." She not only agreed to my terms, but I can't tell you how many people she's told that story to. She couldn't believe how I dictated terms to her with such rigidity (or, alternative reading: how I was clear about exactly what I wanted and could offer). I delivered, it was a minimal effort on both our parts, she was happy with the results, and by being so clear I differentiated myself and built my brand. It's become a story-on-the-street about me. People know I'm efficient, fast, and get things done—and other opportunities have come to me as a result.

My response to this woman's request came partly from boldness. But it also came from my flipping the possible limitations. My thought process went something like this: "I don't have time to do this, but I'd like to, so if I did have the time, how would I organize it?" The proposal I sent her was one that used the path of least resistance, allowing minimum energy for maximum impact. I figured that if she liked it, great. If not, I didn't have time to do it using the normal "by committee" method and would have to pass anyway.

What I did was audacious. But it paid off. Do you spend more of your time in boldness or in fear? Fear interferes with our ability to flip obstacles and take the kinds of risks required to succeed. If you find risk taking difficult, you can flip it.

Here's a bit of help from brain science. The last fifteen years or so have seen an explosion in research on how the brain works. One of the writers in this new field is Rick Hanson, a neuropsychologist who follows the latest brain studies and creates practices to help people deal more effectively with negative beliefs. He feels it's important to understand that throughout our evolutionary history, humans developed what he calls a "negativity bias," which is the brain's tendency to overemphasize the negative in any situation in order to keep us safe. As he's famously remarked, the brain is "Teflon for the positive and Velcro for the negative."

This negativity worked well in the jungle, because if we were wandering around smelling the flowers and didn't notice the tiger chasing us, we wouldn't live to pass on our genes. But it's resulted in a wide range of negative consequences for us in modern life. What's most relevant here is that the negativity bias creates many more negative than positive beliefs about ourselves: "I'm lazy," "I lack willpower," "I'm too shy." These negative thoughts operate below the level of conscious awareness and end up controlling our actions to a much greater degree than we'd like.

Fortunately, says Hanson, we can reverse this negative mental stranglehold by emphasizing the positive in ourselves so that we start to have more positive beliefs. When you catch yourself having a self-limiting thought, challenge yourself to think of something you've done that refutes that thought: the time you spoke to that small group, or engaged someone in your cause, or worked up to your potential. Bring it to mind vividly and hold it for thirty seconds. Hanson says the longer you hold it and the more emotionally stimulating it is, the more your brain will wire it as a good memory to refer back to.

I also love the tool I call "cancel, cancel, cancel." When you catch yourself putting a self-limiting belief out there, say, "Cancel" three times. It brings your attention to the negative thought and tells your mind not to pay attention to it. Kids love this tool as well. I taught it to my nephews and nieces when I heard them make statements like "I can't do that." or "I'm not good at art." When my nephew Finn first caught himself saying he wasn't good at something and then said, "Cancel, cancel, cancel," I was in heaven. It's a huge gift to be able to recognize when you're limiting yourself. Without that recognition it's hard to get on a growth path forward.

Research has shown that one of the key reasons women don't risk following their dreams is that they think they lack the proper background or preparation. We undervalue our capacities and "self-select out" of taking on challenges, says University of California president Janet Napolitano and former head of U.S. Homeland Security. All you have to do, says Napolitano, is to take a close look at "some of these guys ... and ... go—really?"

That's why, in order to succeed as a SheEO, you need to dare to risk. You're doing something you've never done before, so of course you don't know exactly how to do it. Why would you? But somehow, as Napolitano points out, women tend to think they should know everything *before they even attempt something*. And that since everyone else already knows how to do it, how they're feeling is wrong.

Well-known angel investor Daphne Kis agrees. She said she often sees women who feel compelled to get a lot of experience first. This leads them to start their businesses later in life, which puts them further behind their male counterparts. Of course there are true limitations in any situation, but don't add false limitations by assuming that everyone else in the world knows what they're doing and you're the only person who doesn't.

The first step in dealing more effectively with risk is to accept that when we do something for the first time, everyone goes through a stage of not knowing. That's normal. Then look at your pattern of success around risk taking and ask yourself: "What have I done in the past that I can leverage now? How have I dealt with risk before? Where can I go for help? Who can I turn to for support?" It can help to have a base of past success and support from others.

This was true for Anne Gust Brown, the first lady of California. She left a high-powered job as chief administrative officer at the Gap to marry Jerry Brown and then run his campaign for attorney general and later for governor. "I don't know what came over me ... I had to learn everything," she revealed in a newspaper interview. "I had to learn, what is polling, how do you do a TV ad, how do you raise the money? Every day I had to learn something new." People around her told her it was a big mistake to mix the personal and professional. What helped the most, she says, was her husband's confidence in her.

That's one of the benefits of joining a SheEO or other cohort group. You get support from other women to take the leaps you need in order to succeed. You dare more, fear less.

Some people, like me, go headfirst toward what we fear. We take fear as a sign that we have to go after exactly the thing we're afraid of. It's like the title of one of Cheri Huber's books: *If You Have a Fear of Falling, Dive*. Feeling afraid? Go toward it. Go into it. What you fear draws near. It's coming at you anyway, so go forward and meet it.

I did exactly that when I decided that I needed to become a public speaker. I was totally nervous and terrible at it. So in order to get better, I told everyone I knew that I wanted to do public speaking. All of a sudden I was invited to speak in front of twelve hundred people. That first time, my legs were shaking and my voice was quivering. I wasn't great. But I kept on doing it and got better and better, and the fear got less and less. Today, I can speak with confidence and some degree of expertise.

CROSSING THE FEAR THRESHOLD

I recently learned why it feels like such a risk to try something new, which I hope will help you cross more easily over the fear threshold. It comes from Bill Bowen, the creator of psycho-physical therapy. To understand it requires knowing two things about the brain. First, when the part of our brain called the amygdala perceives something potentially painful or unpleasant, it turns on the flight–fight–freeze response, meaning we feel like either running away, fighting, or freezing in place. Second, whenever we anticipate or experience something pleasurable or rewarding, our brain releases dopamine, the feel-good hormone. When we consider taking a risk, the brain switches off dopamine, which then generates a sense of unease in the body. It's the combined result of these two mechanisms that engenders the familiar "Hell, no" response.

After studying the creative process for the past thirty years, Bowen believes that when we consider taking a risk our body-brain moves on a continuum between the fight-or-flight impulse at the one end and the free-flowing expression of creativity at the other. Somewhere on the continuum, writes Linda Graham in *The Wise Brain Bulletin*, "there is a somatic threshold that we feel viscerally in our body, where the body-brain stops us from going forward.... This somatic marker is the disruption of the dopamine, which is letting us know, 'Uh-oh, this is not what was expected.'"

Bowen says that in order to be able to risk and fully engage creatively, we need to notice the marker and understand that it's our body-mind's indication of something new, *not something dangerous*, and thus to override the sense of unease, which will go away once what we're doing becomes familiar and our brains are back to giving us dopamine.

This mechanism explains why my going toward the fear works for me. If you want to try it for yourself, follow these three steps:

1. Notice your fear signal.

2. Evaluate whether it's responding to something truly dangerous or if it's just an indication that your dopamine level has dropped.

3. If it's just your dopamine system, choose to cross the threshold and do the uncomfortable thing. The more you do, the more you learn that daring to risk will bring pleasure and reward. Not to mention greater success as a SheEO!

"I COLLECT TEN NO's EVERY DAY"

One feedback we get most often about the SheEO program is how valuable it is in helping participants reframe their perspectives on failure. After all, to succeed as an entrepreneur we need to be bold and take risks, and inevitably some of those risks won't pan out. And we need to see that this isn't such a terrible thing.

Like most entrepreneurs, I've started several businesses. Some succeeded, and others "failed." I put "failed" in quotes because I don't really see anything I've done as a failure. I can't fail unless I've been bold and taken big risks. If you're stretching yourself, you're bound to encounter failure. That's why I love the quote that heads this section. It's from Jane Roos, who's a SheEO guest speaker and a brilliant fundraiser. Jane has raised over $15 million for Canadian Olympic athletes, most of whom live below the poverty line. For her last campaign she made eight hundred calls asking for money from people she'd never met—and collecting ten no's per day. If she's not, she explains, it means she's not stretching herself enough.

One of my biggest "failures" was impact aggregator Zazengo, which I worked on for five years. When I started, I had this line in mind: "We're the only species on the planet that acts against our own wisdom." I'd hoped there was a way that technology could fundamentally change our behavior by giving us insight into how misaligned our actions are with what we really want. Our first big clients were Walmart and then Johnson & Johnson, who used it to track the sustainability action of their employees. Ultimately, though, for a variety of reasons it didn't work.

Shutting it down was, of course, very hard. I didn't want to fail. I had people I had to let go. I had an investor who wasn't thrilled. And I still believed that the product was needed. With reflection and time, I ended up recognizing that Zazengo had taught me I could sell a technology product to the biggest company in the world. I also learned that it was too ahead of its time. I learned a lot about technology and about what I was still missing on my team. The biggest thing I learned, though, was that it took me too long to let go. I'd lost my energy and enthusiasm, which was a death knell for the company.

In addition to all that, ending Zazengo wasn't a failure because it led to my next chapter, at an innovation center in Canada. There I advised more than five hundred startups, and over that eighteen-month period I started to notice trends and patterns in the next generation of entrepreneurs. And that led me to the rebirth of SheEO. It's a great example of how when one door closes, another always opens.

With the right mental attitude, we can mine our "failure" for maximum learning. I heard a line recently that I love: failure is feedback. That's all it is. When I'm doing something and it doesn't work, that's feedback. It could be that what I'm doing doesn't work for me—it isn't aligned with what inspires me and energizes me. Or it could be that I haven't quite figured out the right model or approach. Or that I haven't got the right partners. Or that my timing is off. Rather than slink into a hole and give up, I look at the situation to see what I can learn. Here are three great questions to help you get the most useful feedback out of any situation that appears to be a failure.

1. What's the lesson here?

2. What's great about having this problem?

3. What's my next action?

Of course you also have to deal with your feelings about what's happened. And one emotion SheEOs need to learn to relate to well is regret. It's easy to say, "Have no regrets," but psychology professor Neal Roese, who wrote a book called *If Only*, says that "what if" and "if only" thinking is actually a biological tool designed to improve our lives. "[Regret is] a key component of a silently effective brain system by which people comprehend reality, learn from mistakes, move forward, and achieve a bettering of their circumstances," he writes. "It is true that you can suffer too many regrets, making it important to leave the past behind and move on with your life. But you can have too few regrets as well. Neglecting the messages of your own emotions can mean persisting in counterproductive behaviors and missing unique opportunities for growth and renewal."

So how should you handle regret? Roese has six suggestions:

1. **Feel the regret and swiftly move on by using it as a springboard to action.** According to Roese, successful entrepreneurs are particularly good at this, using mistakes to vault them into improvements of their products, services, and/or organizations.

2. **Find more than one reason for what happened.** Yes, you failed to make a viable product, but other people were

involved as well, the timing was bad, and so forth. Coming up with possible other factors can help you mine the lesson.

3. **How could this be worse?** Focusing on how what happened could be worse gives you a burst of positive feeling and helps you keep a wider perspective.

4. **Don't spend too much time coming up with all the things you should have done.** It turns out that it's good to think of a few, say three, because it helps you feel in control. But straining to come up with a dozen makes you feel less in control.

5. **Tell someone else, either by writing or talking.** "Telling others can improve health, reduce doctor visits, fortify your immune system, and increase life satisfaction," writes Roese. That's one of the main reasons why a SheEO cohort can be so helpful: she provides a regular way for you to reflect, share experiences with others, and see your situation in a wider context.

6. **Keep your eye on the larger picture.** Because the brain has a tendency to narrow its focus under stress, you can end up overfocusing on the problem and your regret. When you keep your eye on the big picture, on "the overall goals for you personally, for your family, or for your organization ... regret can be brought forward to its highest degree of usefulness."

THE LOVING VOICE

This is one of my favorite practices. It comes from a conversation I once had with Cheri Huber: we were talking about the voices in your head and how hard it is sometimes to turn them off. She said, "Is that voice in your head a loving voice? If so, listen to it. If not, it's probably not yours." Wow! That really helped me to stop listening to a lot of voices I had going on inside me. Now I use this practice not only with myself, but with the people I mentor.

One day I was sitting with a young SheEO. She was telling me how she should have noticed that her business partner, who was handling her company's financials, was incompetent. He'd almost caused their organization to go bankrupt. As I listened to her beat herself up, I asked, "Is that a loving voice you're using toward yourself?" She looked at me, her eyes welled up with tears, and a whole part of her she hadn't known existed came rushing forward with emotion.

Later that night she emailed me saying that for years she'd avoided really learning about the financial aspect of business and had just realized that she'd been limiting her potential by not being financially literate herself. She said she was going to make it her mission to learn all she could about finance as it related to her company. She got a financial mentor and now runs all the books for her burgeoning company. She couldn't see her self-limiting belief and change it until she was kind to herself. Beating herself up had only kept her stuck.

When we speak to ourselves with a loving voice, we create the conditions that allow us to change, to learn as much as we can from what went wrong so that, moving forward, we can have even more of what we truly want.

Let's take advantage of obstacles and flip
them to become the solution.
#IamASheEO

Be clear on the big concept of what you
want—without getting hung up on the details.
#IamASheEO

Pay attention to the energy coming toward you rather
than your notion of what should be coming along.
#IamASheEO

It takes boldness to assume you can have what you want.
The more you assume, the more you will get.
#IamASheEO

Do you spend more of your time in boldness or in fear?
#IamASheEO

Failure is feedback. We can mine those failures
for maximum learnings.
#IamASheEO

When we speak to ourselves with a loving voice, we
create the conditions that allow us to change.
#IamASheEO

PRINCIPLE **6**

FOLLOW THE ENERGY

You will recognize your own path when you come upon it, because you will suddenly have all the energy and imagination you will ever need.

—Jerry Gillies

Sara Blakely is the founder of Spanx, the incredibly successful shapewear company for women. Did you know that she had a huge order from Neiman Marcus before she even knew how she'd mass-produce a critical component of her pantyhose? And that she didn't put the effort into creating a slick website until she got on the *Oprah* show, when she quickly put one together because she needed it?

I love Sara's story because it aligns perfectly with SheEO Principle 6: follow the energy. By this I mean expend the least amount of energy necessary for the maximum impact. In other words, don't spend time creating anything before it's needed, because it might be a waste of energy. As Sara knows, it's all about paying attention to the energy-for-impact ratio.

I've always been obsessed with the energy-for-impact ratio. So much so that I've created companies called KidsNRG and Impactanation. Even my company Zazengo (zazen = awareness, go = action ... moving from awareness to action) was about impact. I firmly believe that the world needs each and every one of us to maximize our impact. In order to do this well, we need to be aware of where and how we're spending our energy. After all, this is our one and only life, and with the world in the sorry shape it is, we each have to be maximally leveraging what we're doing. That's why I love Robert Fritz's concept of the path of least resistance you learned about in the preceding chapter. It's an energy-for-impact strategy.

I think I've focused on this strategy so much because my uncle had chronic fatigue syndrome. It helped me to be cognizant that energy is not endless. That's why I continually ask myself, "How do I make sure my energy-for-impact equation is getting better and better?"

As you know from Principle 3, you can't be someone else and lead. I truly believe that if you're energized by something, it will generally be more successful and lead to more greatness. For me, it's a self-reinforcing spiral: I get energized by energizing others and am energized by being around others having an impact. Which gives me the energy to go out and have a wider impact. If the same is true for you, when you're doing what you can do effortlessly, you actually get energy that spurs you on further.

It's also a good business strategy. As a SheEO, your time and energy are finite resources that need to be used wisely in order to produce the results you want. Often, in the startup phase, you end up doing every-thing—and sometimes focusing on things that aren't that important. But you often won't know that until, after you've done them, you ask yourself, "Did that create an impact? Was it of value?" So to leverage your effectiveness, I want you to push back on the notion that you "have" to do things in a certain way or at a certain time, and to get creative about how things get done.

To truly maximize energy for impact, you have to evaluate every-thing you're doing through this lens. How much energy is any given thing taking? Is the result worth it? How's your energy right now? Is it up, so that you're leaning forward, really engaged? Or is it down, indi-cating that you're not leveraging yourself well? What about the people around you? What's their energy like?

When I'm not energized, I'm not doing my best work. But when I'm in the zone, I can get things done in ten minutes that would otherwise take me hours. If something is energizing me I'm fully alive and focused. When I'm not energized, I'm feeling lazy or bored or frustrated. Clearly that doesn't lead to my best work.

Corporations use the term *engagement* in a way that's similar to how I use *energy*. According to Towers Watson's 2012 *Global Workplace Study*, employee engagement is at an all-time low, with only 35 percent of the full-time employees studied being highly engaged. When you aren't engaged, you aren't productive. As a creator, maker, or entrepreneur, you're in charge of the environment you create for yourself. So it's critical to get yourself fully engaged when you need to be so that you can get the important work done.

This laser focus on energy for impact has led me to create or adopt a number of suggestions relating to many common business activities. In sharing them, I'd like to challenge you to continually monitor your energy and evaluate your impact. If something is really working, go toward it even more. If not, find a new solution.

ENERGY-FOR-IMPACT PERSONAL STRATEGIES

1. ONE THING AT A TIME

In the interest of getting as much done as possible, we've all become furious multitaskers, right? We're texting and reading emails during meetings, scanning Facebook and Twitter while on a conference call ... you know, your multitasking personal favorite. But more and more research is showing that there isn't actually such a thing as multitasking unless one of the tasks is something like walking or eating or emptying the dishwasher. In other words, an automatic, muscle-memory task.

But that's not what most of us are doing. Did you know that when you do two or more cognitive tasks at a time, your energy-for-impact suffers? That's because there's no such thing as multitasking cognitive tasks. Instead, your brain is switching back and forth between them. Even though it feels instantaneous, every shift takes time—up to 40 percent more time than if you'd focused on one thing. Not only that, but your brain has to use what scientists call "cognitive effort," which is draining, meaning we become less mentally sharp. Worst of all, we don't even recognize the negative effects multitasking has on us. In fact, Stanford researcher Clifford Nass discovered that the very people who claim to be the best multitaskers were actually the *worst* at things like organizing information, switching between tasks, and discerning significance—all crucial capacities for successful SheEOs. These multitaskers made more mistakes and could remember less than non-multitaskers. And other studies have shown that employees who check their emails frequently are less productive than those who check fewer times during the day.

David Rock, author of *Your Brain at Work*, argues that to be high-performing leaders, we must learn to treat our brain—and particularly the prefrontal cortex, which is responsible for abstract thinking, making decisions, predicting the future, and regulating our behavior—as a precious, limited resource. He likens it to a battery. When we're aware of what drains the battery (like multitasking) as well as what recharges it (sleep, exercise, food), we can make wise choices about how we work.

Moreover, throwing more time and effort at something doesn't necessarily produce good results. Studies have shown that thinking past the point of tiredness decreases decision-making capacity by up to 500 percent. We need daily breaks, like going to the gym or taking a walk, to recharge and refresh; they can help us get our work done in less time. It may sound counterintuitive, but we can increase productivity by taking time off.

It comes down to the energy-for-impact ratio. To make sure I'm getting the highest-quality results for my effort, I now do one thing at a time and monitor my energy during the day—that way, whatever I'm doing, I'm giving it my best brain power.

2. ROCKS FIRST

As a SheEO, you have hundreds of demands, big and small, on your time every week. There's so much more you could do than you have time to do it in. And if you're not careful, you can spend so much time on the urgent that you never get to what's most important. One way to make sure you're focusing on the right things is to do "rocks first." The metaphor comes from a widely circulating thought experiment.

Take a large jar and some rocks, pebbles, and sand. If you put the pebbles and sand in the jar first, there's no room for the rocks. But if you put the rocks in first, the pebbles and sand easily fit around the rocks. In business terms, the rocks are your clear priorities—those things you've decided are the key drivers to success. If you focus on those, then the smaller things will move around to fill the space left over. It might sound obvious to focus on the important stuff, but it's easy to lose sight of the rocks and end up buried under a mountain ᴏ. pebbles and sand.

Gino Wickman, author of *Traction*, suggests first setting a clear picture of where you want to be in three years. You've already done that in the preceding chapter when you established your desired result. Wickman proposes that you then create three to seven ninety-day rocks—clear objectives that you believe will most contribute right now to achieving your vision. In this way, he says, you "create a 90-Day World. Rather than being overwhelmed by the monumental task of accomplishing your vision, this allows you to break it down into bite-sized chunks." Depending on the size of your organization, your company will have rocks, your leadership team will have rocks, and every employee will have rocks. Every ninety days, you evaluate your progress and set up new rocks. As Wickman puts it, "The way you move the company forward is one 90-day period at a time." (For more about the procedures that can help you gain traction, take a look at his website at http://eosworldwide.com.)

I like Wickman's focus on rocks and on ninety days because it emphasizes first a laser focus on your goals, and then the time you need to assess your energy for impact and where the path of least resistance is emerging. You're never more than three months away from making a shift.

3. DO A WEEKLY AIRPLANE VIEW

Organizational guru David Allen, author of *Getting Things Done*, proposes a regularly scheduled "airplane view"—meaning that you set aside time at the beginning or end of every week to take a higher-level view of what you're doing. Most likely you've been busy all week having meetings and checking things off your to-do list. With an airplane view, you get above the specifics and take a look at the whole. If you've created three to seven rocks, are you moving them all forward? What have you done to chip away at each one? Which needs more attention in the week coming up? Which needs less? What other issues, the pebbles and sand, demand your attention now?

If you don't take regular time to view what you're doing as a whole, you can easily lose track of something significant. Think, too, about your energy for impact. What are you doing that's really working so that you should do more of it? What's not? How could you turn that around?

Research has shown that very basic diagrams are highly useful to the brain in creating understanding and recall. That's why M.J. suggests you create a visual of your rocks. When it's time for the airplane view, take out that visual, look at each rock, and think about what you've done and what needs to happen next. That way you can keep it all moving forward in the most impactful way.

ENERGY-FOR-IMPACT MEETINGS

1. TRACK THE ENERGY IN EVERY MEETING

Tracking energy is gold. I do it during meetings, whether they're with my team, a group of clients, or one-on-one. It's about paying attention to what's happening energy-wise with each person and the dynamic between people. Is the energy up or is it down? What impact are you having? Is that the impact you want? Then I call out what I'm noticing: "The energy seems to have gone down, so let's stop for now." Or "Richard, you suddenly seem disengaged. What's going for you?" Or "I notice my energy is going up around this. Let me take it and run with it."

When I call out what I see, it gives people permission to tell themselves and one another the truth about what's going on for them, which minimizes time wasted on unproductive meetings and/or disengaged participants. It brings to the surface whatever's going on below the conversation so that roadblocks can be more easily eliminated. In customer and client conversations, it can help you figure out if there's a real possibility to work together or not, regardless of what the person is saying. It makes every meeting more efficient. When you note that someone doesn't seem really present, that's usually a gift—because by surfacing it, you're giving the other person permission to say what's true for him or her. In my experience, that person almost always has something to give that's just not being pulled out.

When you track energy in meetings, you avoid the terrible "We just have to get through these twenty-five agenda items" syndrome, which makes people ignore their own energy in order to grind it out. I was once in a meeting when someone said, "Let's just keep this high level today." Translated, that meant no one had done what they were supposed to do since the last meeting, so "Let's just rehash things without calling anyone on it." But when you're a SheEO, you have no time to waste. If no progress has been made, cancel the meeting and come back when you've actually got something crucial to talk about.

Remember, when you're energized by something, it will generally be more successful than when you're not. So why ignore the feedback about what's not working for you or others? If your energy is low, maybe you need to take a break by having a nap or going for a walk. Or you're thinking about an issue too much and need to just let it go. But maybe your energy is down because you're not really behind this particular idea.

We all have times when we have to get stuff done. But why not have an energizing way of doing it?

2. BE AN EXCELLENT AGENDA SETTER

When I learned this tool for rapid, just-in-time agenda setting, I was in heaven. You don't create an agenda in advance. At the beginning of a meeting, you ask everyone what they need to talk about and how long they need: Richard, three minutes to update us on the conference schedule; Vicki, two minutes to get feedback on the media release, and so on. In this way, only what's urgent or important gets discussed. You also get skilled at time management, knowing how long it will take to get the outcome you want. People tend to attribute too much time to each task, but with practice you learn that it can take far less time. I've had really energizing, highly valuable meetings where we've gone through twenty agenda items in under ten minutes.

3. IDENTIFY OBJECTIVES BEFORE YOU START

Whether you call it a desired result, a goal, or an objective, every time you meet with anyone to discuss anything, you should first establish your destination: "To make a decision on whether to rent office space." "To establish the conditions under which we'd work together." "To decide on a project management system." This way, every person involved understands where you're trying to end up. If you don't take the time to establish that at the outset, people can talk at cross purposes, conversations can wander, and you can waste vast amounts of time. But with a clear objective, it's easier to tell if you're going off on tangents and easier to recognize when you've arrived.

It's also important to be clear on what others want out of the meeting. That's because we often make assumptions. I, for example, err on the side of fixing things; my default is to action everything. In the past I've often assumed that if you're coming to me, you want something to be fixed. But sometimes people just want to vent—and if that's the case, it's good to know so that I can be a sounding board.

I do this in every conversation, even one-on-ones. I first ask what the other person's objective is, which helps me understand what she or he is looking for so that I can help create that outcome. And by sharing what I'm looking for, even if my outcome is different from theirs, we're both more likely to get what we want. Otherwise, it's easy for one person to feel it's been a successful meeting while the other person is left dissatisfied.

4. USE "I PROPOSE"

I first learned this technique at Seattle's Software Development Boot-camp, which is run by my good friend John Rae-Grant. So often people will spend hours in a meeting, having entire conversations about a wide variety of topics, only to leave at the end unclear as to whether they've actually made any decisions. Or they have different ideas of what decisions have been made. One person, usually the leader, says something like, "We made ten decisions," while other people, usually those who didn't get heard, say, "What are you talking about? I didn't agree to that." It's a huge energy and time suck. "I propose" greatly reduces, if not eliminates, that confusion.

What it means is that you don't make any suggestions without beginning with the words "I propose": "I propose we engage this marketing firm." "I propose we use this logo." Then people vote by putting up their hands. And you watch how they do it—for example, if some people's hands are only halfway up, it's a way of noticing the energy of what's going on and focusing in on those people: "You don't seem quite in. What are your concerns? What would work for you?"

I've worked with a lot of people who, at first, think this process suggestion is a waste of time. But after they try it a few times, they realize that it really speeds things up.

5. STOP SITTING AROUND TALKING

Where did we get the idea that in order to have a productive meeting we need to sit around in a big group and talk through every issue? Particularly in the brainstorming phase of an idea, it can be much more efficient to write your thoughts down on sticky notes or a piece of paper and then discuss. Try it both ways—talking and writing—and see how much faster the discussion goes when you've written down your ideas first. Or split up into subgroups to work on different aspects of the issue and then come together. I do this even in groups as small as four people, because, again, it's more efficient. Take a walk and talk about the issue with one other person. Then return and share.

In addition, be clear about who really needs to be in the room, for what input, at what point, and for how long. Get vigilant about how to get the most out of everyone in a way that uses their strengths and builds trust in the group. Not everyone needs to sit through everything if it doesn't apply to them or they can't add anything useful.

ENERGY-FOR-IMPACT
BRAINSTORMING

1. WHEN YOU'RE STUCK, CALL A FIVE-MINUTE BRAINSTORM

If you feel you're banging your head against a wall and can't come up with a solution on your own, enlist others to brainstorm with you for five minutes. You can do it live or via Skype or Google hangouts. Each person has a bunch of sticky notes and five minutes to write down every idea they have for how to solve your problem. Then you collect the ideas, thank them, and everyone goes back to what they were doing. Especially if you're working with a team, this quick injection of energy definitely improves the impact you're trying to have. It also engages the other people so that now they're thinking about your issue. You may find that they end up coming back with more ideas because their thinking has been percolating since the brainstorm.

We do this in the SheEO program. We interject five-minute brainstorms throughout each session so that each SheEO gets a chance to have everyone's brain working on an issue of importance to her. In fact, this is one of the most highly requested activities in the program. Not only does it yield great value in a very short period of time, but you also get to know who in your cohort is good at providing what kind of information.

Five minutes is all you really need, I've found. You don't have to put seven hours into a problem to get a great result. In fact, the worst thing in the world is to sit for an hour. It doesn't energize anyone, and it doesn't get you maximum energy for impact.

2. DO IT GOOGLE STYLE

Mary Zhu pioneered this brainstorming method at the University of Michigan. Originally developed by a Firefox co-founder, it's been used regularly at Google to come up with new ideas. It's best done in groups of three, whether online or in person.

1. Each person has a stack of sticky notes.

2. Create three designs/ideas that solve the problem.

3. Spend only one minute on each design/idea.

4. Pass your design/idea to the person on your right.

5. Add to the designs/ideas just passed to you.

6. Wash, rinse, repeat.

This process is a great way to get ideas out quickly, and it'll give you valuable practice in adding to others' ideas.

3. FLOAT THE BLUE BALLOON

How many times have you sat around trying to come up with an innovative idea and nothing pops—until you give up? Current research on creativity confirms that in order to have a breakthrough idea, you need to stop "trying" and let it go. My friend and author Dr. Dawna Markova calls it "floating the blue balloon." Ask your question, visualize putting it in a blue balloon, and watch it float away. Then, when you least expect it, the perfect solution pops in. How is it that although we've all experienced this phenomenon, we still tend not to trust that it really is how our brains work? Instead we try to push through. We focus harder. We force ourselves to sit, regardless of what the energy is, and try to come up with the creative idea we're looking for.

But honestly, we're wasting our energy. Innovative solutions won't come by "trying." Here's why. The latest in neuroscience says that our thinking isn't controlled by specific *regions* of the brain but rather by various brain *networks*. There are three networks involved in creativity. The Attentional Control network is activated when you "pay attention," focusing like a laser beam on a problem or task. The Imagination network is activated when you remember the past, think about the future, and imagine alternatives in general. And the Attentional Flexibility network monitors both external events and your internal stream of consciousness. It passes the baton between the Attentional Control network and the Imagination network.

The latest research suggests that in order to have out-of-the-box ideas, you need to reduce activation of the Attentional Control network and increase activation of the other two. How do you do that? Stop trying! Go do something else, trusting that your brain will be working on the issue below the level of your conscious attention.

What I love about this research is that it confirms my belief that you can't just throw more time and effort at things to get a good result. As someone once said to me, "Trying is very trying."

That's why, when I find I'm stuck and a creative solution isn't coming, I get clear on the question I want to float, either by myself or with others. And then I imagine the question floating off in the blue balloon. I let it float, knowing the answer will emerge, and then I go for a walk, go to a movie—anything but think of the thing I'm trying to solve.

ENERGY-FOR-IMPACT BUSINESS DEVELOPMENT

1. BE AGILE

There's a principle in technology development these days called MVP, or minimum viable product. You create just enough features to generate enough value for your customer so that you can get feedback on your idea. Then you iterate based on what you've learned, adding features according to customer need and value. It's called agile development.

What's interesting to me about agile development is that I've always built my businesses that way, even those that didn't necessarily have a technology component. That's also what Sara Blakely, founder of Spanx, did in the opening story of this chapter. For one new venture I co-founded, we had a narrative for the company and nothing else. No logo, no website, no one-pager, no business plan, no pitch deck. Just an idea. Then we went to see what kind of response we'd get.

In the first meeting, the client was interested and we got a contract. Cool. That worked. Second meeting, got another client. Then, as we broadened our reach, people started asking for a one-pager. As someone who wants to do only what's absolutely crucial, I rarely create something before it's requested. You save a tremendous amount of energy (and money, frankly) by not creating collateral that isn't needed or, based on feedback, ends up being wrong. In that particular startup we had four clients and were in existence for six months before we even created a logo.

I know this flies in the face of most business school and mentorship advice. You need a business plan. You need stationery and logos and a website. Right? But why? I've seen people waste thousands, sometimes hundreds of thousands of dollars (not to mention all those person hours) creating an elaborate back-end infrastructure for a business idea no one wanted. They could have found that out very quickly if they'd gone out to the market beforehand and tested the concept. Or they could have tweaked their idea based on feedback so that when they did create the website or product it would already have traction and therefore be more likely to succeed.

One thing you can know for sure is that your five-year business plan is highly unlikely to happen the way you think it will. As Steve Blank and Bob Dorf, grandfathers of the lean startup movement, wrote, "No business plan survives first contact with customers." Here are some other pearls of wisdom from Blank on the topic:

- Business plans are the leading cause of startup death.
- Rapidly changing markets require continuous business model iteration/customer development.

- There are no facts inside your building, so get outside and get some.

- Few if any investors read your business plan to see if they're interested in your business. They're a lot more interested in what you've learned.

I couldn't agree more with this advice. Thankfully, people are increasingly coming to realize that big, bulky business plans aren't worth the effort. Ten years ago you couldn't get an investor meeting without one. Now you're unlikely to have any top investor even read it. It's important to show that you can think through a scenario—which, after all, is what a business plan is—but spending hours and hours on it is a waste of time.

2. STOP TRYING TO BE ALL THINGS TO ALL PEOPLE

As I talked about in Principle 1, the long tail means it isn't necessary that everyone needs or wants what you're offering. Chances are, if you're sufficiently differentiated, you'll have a big-enough pool of interested people to be successful. It's all about getting clear on who you are and what you're looking for—and not trying to be everything to everyone.

I learned this lesson the hard way. When I ran KidsNRG I spent years rewriting the website every two months and driving my team crazy. That was because, although half of those who came to our website said, "I've waited my whole life for a company like this and I want to work with you," the other half said, "I've read everything on your site and I still have no idea what you do." Instead of seeing it as a gift that our site was screening out those who didn't get us, I kept trying to capture that second half. Not only did I not need them, but in trying to be all things to all people, I was diluting what made the website work for the first half. I spent tons of time trying to convince them of my message rather than understanding that there are people who are my audience and there are people who are not.

Through decades of agile business development, I've learned that if I have to convince somebody of something, I might as well forget it. And what a gift it is to have people quickly not get me, because then it's easy to walk away! I no longer try to convince anyone of anything.

Instead I search for the customers, investors, partners, and employees who run toward me with excitement. They're the best people to work with, because I can learn with them, I can share with them, and we have a strong values connection.

Back in Principle 2 I quoted a line from dot-com pioneer Joe Kraus, and I think his observation bears repeating here: "The twentieth century was about dozens of markets of millions of consumers. The twenty-first century is about millions of markets of dozens of consumers." You don't need to be all things to all people; you just need to find your tribe.

3. WHO ARE THE FIVE PEOPLE LIKE YOU?

In Principle 4 I talked about the "five people" approach in the context of networking. But it works for business development, too. Whenever I meet someone who's interested in what I'm doing, who "gets it," I ask if they can connect me to five people like them. That way I increase the likelihood of meeting the kinds of clients (or customers or funders) who'll be attracted to what I'm doing. It's the easiest way I know to build my tribe.

4. USE THE ONE-MEETING RULE

I used to have a four-meeting rule, which is that if something significant wasn't happening within four meetings—a partnership, say, or a business deal—I wouldn't meet with that person again. I don't think I have that rule anymore—I probably have a one-meeting rule now. I'm being a bit facetious, because of course not everything is instantaneous. There are things you have to plant and then wait to come back to you. But if you're meeting over and over, not getting where you want to go and feeling that it's difficult, why not choose to put your energy elsewhere so that you can discover the path of least resistance?

This applies especially to the startup stage. I recently met a SheEO who got a major investor at minute eighteen of an hour-long meeting. That doesn't happen every day, but the energy-for-impact principle encourages you to search for those types of experiences rather than spend six months and hundreds of hours trying to make something happen with people who don't really get you.

ENERGY-FOR-IMPACT FUNDING

1. DON'T GO FOR FIFTY FUNDERS WHEN ONE WILL DO

When I was raising money for Zazengo, I was told that for social ventures most people invest in the $50,000 range. I was looking to raise $1 million, so that's a lot of people to talk to, a lot of paperwork, and a lot of investors to manage. After all, every one of those investors will tend to call you regularly to find out what's happening and to send you three people they want you to talk to or employ. It takes a huge amount of energy.

I think I had seven or eight yeses when I thought of calling a particular woman. We hadn't spoken for fifteen years. We had a wide-ranging talk about the state of the world, what I'd been doing and learning, my vision, my passion, common experiences we'd had. We talked for an hour. At the end of the phone call she said, "I've been waiting for you." And she took the whole round for $1 million.

When I talk about funding with my SheEO cohorts, I tell them this story as an example of how it's possible to get that one perfect values-aligned person who's been waiting their whole life to give money to you. They laugh and say, "That only happens to you." "Ah," I reply, "but what if it was possible for you?"

There's a great Thai proverb that I love: "Someone out there needs you. Live your life so that they can find you." I often think of this when I'm in need of funding. Someone out there with money, whether in the form of investment or philanthropy, is looking for a person who lights them up, who makes them feel good about their contribution, and who's passionate about what they're doing. They're out there. Live your life so that they can find you.

2. FIND YOUR VALUES FIT

There are "rules" to the funding game as it's being played now. In Silicon Valley, for example, if your financial model doesn't project a year-five revenue of at least $100 million, you won't get funded. I experienced this myself. I was going through a pitch with VCs and everyone was nodding along—until I got to slide seventeen (I know, that's one *long* deck; I wouldn't do that today) and my column five had $68 million in revenue. Deal breaker, they said. Not ambitious enough.

At first I thought, "Really? You do realize that these are projections. So if I change my number you'll listen, and if I don't you won't?" Then I realized that I don't want funders like that. I'm not going to pretend to do something just because someone has made up a rule of thumb. That's not my game.

Thankfully, change is in the air. We're now seeing an emerging crop of impact investors who are interested in playing the game differently because they recognize that the model is fundamentally broken—and who'd want to create a funding model where you expect nine out of every ten of your investments to fail? That's the current VC financing model.

As an entrepreneur, you don't need to follow that old model, because otherwise you're just competing for the same limited pool of money in a game that's not yours, in a way that's not sustaining, and with people who expect you to work 24/7. Instead, the more unique you are, the likelier you are to attract funders precisely because of that uniqueness. There are philanthropists and impact investors all over the world with billions of dollars looking for a home. It may be a bit of a needle in a haystack to find them, but they're out there. And today people are helping to curate these investors and investees to make finding one another easier. My good friend Suzanne Biegel, for instance, just launched collaboratewomenandgirls.com, which aggregates all the stakeholders (investors, programs, philanthropists) that back women who are building products and services to support women and girls. Have a look at their website to see the resources available to you.

Follow the energy: expend the least amount
of energy necessary for the maximum impact.
#IamASheEO

Is your energy-for-impact equation always
getting better?
#IamASheEO

How can we get, and stay, in the zone?
Lean toward energy.
#IamASheEO.

There is no such thing as multitasking
cognitive tasks. Focus your energy.
#IamASheEO

Throwing more time and effort at something
doesn't necessarily produce good results.
Follow the energy.
#IamASheEO

What woman would create a funding model
where you expect nine out of every ten of your
investments to fail? We won't.
#IamASheEO

PRINCIPLE

7

INTEGRATION IS
THE NEW BALANCE

*You must learn to be still in the midst of activity
and to be alive in repose.*

—Indira Gandhi

A fortysomething business owner recently told me that after a year of intense work, she'd taken a week off to rest, restore, and reflect— only to receive a call from one of her male advisers saying that taking time off was the wrong thing to do. Outraged, she replied, "This is exactly the company I want to create, one where we work hard *and* take time for integration. I've come back with a whole new perspective that'll benefit what we're doing and that otherwise I never would have had."

Like this woman, SheEOs are at the forefront of the movement to take charge of our own destinies, and that includes redefining when and how we work. It doesn't mean we don't work hard—we often put in long hours—but that we seek to work in a new way that integrates all of who we are and enables us to make the wisest choices.

My guess is that flexibility is a key reason you've chosen to be a SheEO rather than hooking your star to a large corporation. You're not alone. A 2011 study conducted by *More* magazine found that, of the five hundred women surveyed, aged thirty-five to sixty, two out of three would rather have more free time than a bigger paycheck. Only a quarter of them said they're working toward their next promotion, and three out of four—73 percent—said they wouldn't apply for their boss's job owing to the office politics, the stress, and the lack of flexibility that goes along with such positions. Women polled by the website Ladies Who Launch cite freedom, flexibility, and control as the top reasons for starting businesses, with creativity, fulfillment, and passion coming in second and money third. Finally, in a 2013 iVillage study of fifteen hundred working women, a whopping 89 percent of respondents said that they defined career success as the flexibility to balance life and work.

I'm not a big fan of the word *balance*. I think it creates a false belief in an achievable equilibrium, whereas in reality we're in a constant state of flux that moves the pendulum back and forth. In some weeks I'm totally loaded with activities; in others I'm restoring myself to deal with the next wave of craziness. So the word I prefer is *integration*. And that's why it's Principle 7.

Integration is crucial because, as you know firsthand, it's impossible to keep up with everything. There's just too much coming at you. The speed at which we operate today is unbelievable, with almost everyone reacting to what's arriving next in their inbox, having no time to integrate or reflect on what it means and how it might affect them or their business. The pace isn't sustainable—either for your well-being or for your capacity to be a great leader.

We're all suffering from information overload, which, according to Angelika Dimoka, director of the Center for Neural Decision Making at Temple University, actually inhibits our ability to make good choices and effective decisions. Not a good situation for those of us running a business! Her research shows that as the amount of input increases, the executive function that controls rational thinking in our brain switches off and anxiety and frustration soar as the emotional centers of the brain come on stronger. We get more and more upset and stuck.

To make matters worse, a growing science of decision making has revealed that an unconscious system in our brain actually guides many of our decisions, and that it can be sidelined by too much input. And to add insult to injury, it's shown that new ideas, insights, and out-of-the box solutions need to percolate below the level of awareness before they can emerge—something that's increasingly difficult when information keeps flooding in and we don't take time to turn off.

CLAIM TIME TO BE STILL

As members of the SheEO movement, we can reverse this trend and reclaim the reflection time we need in order to make wise choices for ourselves, our organizations, and the planet. We can create space to step back from all the stuff coming at us and ask, "What am I noticing about what's going on? What am I learning?" When you take the time to integrate, you have the opportunity to design or redesign how you're acting and being, the chance to actually create what you want rather than being stuck in firefighting mode. It's true that the fires are burning. They may even be blazing. But you'll never truly get above and beyond them unless you take time out.

I believe in this so strongly that in most of the companies I've created, we've committed to taking one day a week in which there are no client meetings and we can reflect individually and together. Obviously, depending on the kind of business you run, that might not be possible. Does the whole concept of stepping out regularly sound crazy to you? Impossible? But what *could* be possible?

When I asked my uncle what he'd do differently if he lived his life over again, he said two things. First, that he'd take Fridays off to integrate everything he'd been learning, to read and reflect. And second, that he'd make vacations mandatory every quarter for at least a week to remind himself that he's not as important as he thinks he is. "The business won't fall apart if you leave for a week," he proclaimed. Wise advice that I've tried to follow ever since.

If you have a hard time getting people on board in your company, you might want to try something we at KidsNRG did to my brother Matt years ago. He's exceptionally diligent, and had gotten into a cycle where he thought he couldn't get away and so wouldn't take his quarterly vacation. As an owner in the company, you need to model the behavior you want or people won't follow it. So we phoned his friend and asked if he'd go on vacation with Matt. Then we manufactured a meeting out at the airport with an important venture capitalist who was flying into town. We called all of Matt's clients to tell them what we were doing, and they thought it was a great idea—in fact, it actually enhanced our brand with several clients who wished they worked at a company that would do something like that.

Matt got to the airport, saw his friend, and realized what was up. Then he called me, furious, to say he couldn't go; he had too much work to do. I told him that we'd already talked to all his clients and that it was okay. About half an hour later I got another call from the airport bar: it was a much happier Matt, thanking us for the intervention. Sometimes we need our cohort and/or team to remind us that it's possible to take care of ourselves.

This is such a hard lesson for most people to get. I remember reading once about M. Scott Peck, the author of *The Road Less Traveled*. He was explaining how people often asked him how he accomplished so much in a day. He said it was possible because he first took a couple of hours every morning to do nothing. His questioner would always say, "Oh, but I could never do that! I've got too much to do." Most of us believe that only by working longer and harder can we succeed.

Ironically, that belief has only gotten stronger with the proliferation of our always-on devices. But that can be dangerous. It turns out that iPads, iPods, and iPhones train our brains to favor the urgent over the important. We start to believe that if we don't answer this one email or phone call immediately, all hell will break loose. The technology itself—its *bing, bing, bing, bing, bing* nature—is creating a sense of emergency in our minds, making us believe that we must respond as if a crisis were at hand.

Part of what's so challenging about taking time out to integrate has to do with the way our brains are structured. The stress response hasn't evolved to keep up with the new challenges of the twenty-first century. As I talked about earlier, it was designed millennia ago to keep us safe from physical dangers—a tiger appears on the path, and our body/mind automatically prepares to fight, flee, or freeze and hope it doesn't see us. But our brains don't differentiate well between true threats—a car about to run you over—and perceived threats—that email or text *bing*. It goes into emergency mode either way, narrowing our focus to perceive only the potential danger and blocking out everything else. In reality, that text isn't likely to be a true emergency, but unfortunately, our body/mind is responding as if it were.

That's why we have to take charge—because otherwise this automatic biological response will continue to run us. We've bought into the model of a 24/7 world. But it's broken. It's not making anyone healthy or happy. You have your own business because you want to live differently—so that you'll have the flexibility to change the rules.

If this is hard for you, try an assignment that M.J. gives her SheEOs who are stuck in this emergency state of mind. For a week, choose a set period of time, let's say between nine p.m. and seven a.m., during which you turn off all your devices. Then see what happens as a result. Are there a million more fires? One client whom M.J. gave this assignment to called back to say, "There was no difference in the outside world—I just answered in the morning rather than at night and got to avoid all the meaningless back and forths with everyone weighing in. And inside of me, it was so much better. I actually had a little time to myself before I went to bed, plus I got an hour more of sleep!"

Remember, we constructed this always-on world, and we can change it. Just because you have a tool to communicate with doesn't mean you have to use it. And here's a bonus—the fact that you're an advocate for integration is a differentiator. When I tell people that our company takes a day a week to reflect, their usual response is "Really? That's so cool. I'd love to work for a company like that." It creates energy and excitement around you and your organization. As I've said before, being different brings you customers and employees who want that difference. Like the business owner who pushed back on the adviser criticizing her time off, don't worry about the people who say, "You shouldn't/can't do that." Concentrate on those who'll show up expressly for that difference.

So now that you believe in the need for time to integrate, let's look at what you could be reflecting on.

HOW'S THAT WORKING FOR YOU?

I love this phrase, and used it for years before I learned that it's one of Dr. Phil's signature expressions. It goes to the heart of what we could be doing when we reflect—assessing what we've been doing so that we can improve.

When you establish a desired result, you're setting an intention. And intention is a powerful draw to help you get where you want to go. But that's only part of the process. You've got to regularly check in with yourself on how you're doing in relationship to your intention. Failure to do this is why a lot of people stay stuck where they are. They just keep doing the same thing over and over, believing that they just need to apply more elbow grease to get where they want to go. If you reach your personal and professional goals, you have to stop and evaluate what's going on: "What's working? What's not? What can I start to tweak in order to be more successful? How should I shift how I'm acting and being?" The same is true with your business.

As you ask yourself these questions, I hope you're using the loving voice you learned about in Principle 6. Because it's only in a spirit of non-judgment that learning can happen. If you beat yourself up—"Why haven't I done what I said I'd do? What's wrong with me? Why am I such a failure?"—you're "reflecting" in a way that creates a downward spiral of shame, stuckness, and inertia.

But when you're asking in a mode of learning, you can notice what you've done to leverage your successes and find creative solutions to get back on track when you need to. For instance, if you promised yourself to reflect for an hour a day and you haven't done it once in two weeks, using a loving voice, you can think, "I'm out of balance. What's going on? What am I holding on to that I really can let go of? What's standing in my way?"

Self-reflection is such a powerful learning tool that almost every day I look at what worked and what didn't so that I can shift it the next day. For instance, "I'm writing proposals that I don't want to be writing. How could I get clients who don't require those kinds of things?" "I'm not spending enough time with my husband, so how can I get more time for that?" Everything is a feedback loop. It's a continual process of letting go of the things that aren't serving you, things that may have been right just the day before. The more you reflect, the more you can develop yourself to your fullest and bring that fullness to every venture you engage in.

There are all kinds of ways to reflect. You can do it while driving to or from work. If, like me, you have a partner who you can talk things through with and who's non-judgmental, that's a real blessing. I also have mounds of journals that I've used for self-reflection. It doesn't matter how you do it, just that you do it.

WHAT ARE YOU WORKING ON?

If, upon reflection, you realize that there's something in yourself you want to change, there are all kinds of ways to support that. One is to enlist other people. The more you have others helping you with what you're working on, the faster you'll get to your path, right? Well, yes—under the right conditions.

One technique we use in our team is to each answer the "What are you working on?" question and then request support. Recently my answer was "I'm working on being a graceful leader. When I'm not being a graceful leader, I'm controlling and grumpy and fear-based. And when I'm not being graceful, here's what you can say to remind me of how I truly want to be." Notice that I chose the specific words I wanted to hear. So now my teammates ask, "Are you being graceful? Is that the way you want to be a leader?" If you do ask others for help, make sure you're thoughtful about how, when, and where you want feedback. Having others help you get where you want to go makes for faster progress than doing it on your own, but only if it's done in the spirit of growth and doesn't shame you.

Visual reminders are also good. In our company, we each have over our desk a piece of paper stating what we're working on in ourselves and what support we want from one another. This helps each of us keep it front and center.

Here's a way to remember that doesn't involve other people. I recently bought a bracelet that came with an alphabet whose individual letters you can click into the chain. I put in the word *graceful*, and now I look at it ten times a day. It helps me remember. It's about experimenting with different ways to keep your attention on your intention.

What about bringing to your attention changes you need to make that are currently below your level of conscious awareness? For those, I suggest two techniques: the 90 Percent Rule and the What Advice Are You Giving Others? tool. Both are ways to gain feedback about needed growth.

1. THE 90 PERCENT RULE

This rule says that 90 percent of what you see in someone else is really about you. That's because so much of what humans do involves projecting their thoughts and feelings onto others. So if something's bugging you about someone else, there's probably a message in there about you.

I remember the denial I felt the first time I heard this. "Ninety per-cent! No way. That other person is a total nightmare. I'm not like that!" But when I really looked deeply into what was going on, I realized that what was bothering me about the other person really was something I didn't like about myself. It was just easier to see it in them. Since then, I always try to look at what could be true for me in whatever it is that's annoying or frustrating me about someone else.

2. WHAT ADVICE ARE YOU GIVING OTHERS?

I love this one. It's very simple. You just notice the advice you're giving other people—"Oh, gee, for the tenth time this week I just told someone they need to lighten up and have more fun"—and think about how whatever you're saying applies to you—"Huh, I guess I need to lighten up myself."

INTEGRATION IS ABOUT SELF-CARE, TOO

Integration isn't only about mining your experiences for how you can learn and grow. It's also about treating yourself as an integrated human being—with physical, mental, emotional, and spiritual dimensions. This, too, is the beauty of being a SheEO. In far too many workplaces, people are treated as minds only and encouraged to ignore their phys-ical, emotional, and spiritual well-being. But when you create your own workplace, you can do it differently. You can encourage yourself and others to take good care of themselves. *Self-care* isn't a dirty word. You at your optimal best is what's needed to achieve greatness.

This is such an important learning for women in particular to get. Far too often, we sacrifice our own well-being for the sake of others, whether it's other people or our organizations. We SheEOs can be at the forefront of changing that damaging point of view.

I like to use the practice M.J. wrote about in her book *Surviving Change You Didn't Ask For*. It's based on the book *The Power of Full Engagement* by Jim Loehr and Tony Schwartz. In their book, Loehr and Schwartz make the point that working people need to treat themselves just as high-performance athletes do in order to have the stamina to perform at their peak. Athletes have strategies both for extending themselves (by lifting weights, for instance) and for recovery (resting, for instance). Likewise, to have maximum energy, we need regular extension and recovery strategies in all four domains of our existence: physical, mental, emotional, and spiritual.

Take some time to do it right now. Think about each domain—physical, mental, emotional, and spiritual—and write down what you're doing that's stretching you in that place and what you're doing to recover. Then, on a scale of one to ten, rate yourself on how well you're doing in each category, with one being very low and ten being extremely high.

Here are mine.

MENTAL

Extend: Learn something new every week. Be in discussion regarding the latest trends in my favorite subjects. Spend time in conversation with wise people.

Restore: Write blog posts. Draw my learnings to have them come out in non-verbal ways.

PHYSICAL

Extend: Get regular exercise. Walk to work.

Restore: Take time to wind down at night. Stretch. Get a weekly massage.

EMOTIONAL

Extend: Clear up any dangling relationship issues with family, friends, co-workers.

Restore: Journal on how I'm feeling, using stream of consciousness. Draw.

SPIRITUAL

Extend: Meditate and do quantum jumps regularly.

Restore: Watch videos. Discuss what I'm feeling with Richard.

When I first started doing this, I had a really hard time with the "restore" part. I'm great at extending myself. I push myself hard emotionally, mentally, spiritually, and physically, but I don't always pay attention to restoring myself. I think I wrote down "Have a bath at night to chill out" as my restore, in every category. Over time I've played with expanding each area.

Your strategies will be different from mine. That's okay. Just note them. There's no one right way. Then use the information you've discovered to make a plan for self-care.

I also use this tool with my team. At the end of each week we do a summary: "Here were my physical, spiritual, mental, and emotional goals for the week. Here's how I far I got toward them and what worked and what didn't." In this way we help one another along.

IT'S ALL ABOUT A LEARNING MINDSET

In his book *Innovation and Entrepreneurship*, management consultant Peter F. Drucker claims that as we move into an entrepreneurial society, everyone must continue to learn new things throughout their lifetime and to "take responsibility for their learning, their own self-development, and their own careers." I couldn't agree more. At the heart of the SheEO philosophy is the belief that not just business but life itself is all about learning and growing.

Of course you're going to make mistakes; of course you're going to make wrong choices—even if this isn't your first entrepreneurial venture. But with time for reflection, you harvest all the learnings from your experience, persist in getting better, and become wiser and more successful as a result.

This can be harder for women than it is for men. As I talked about earlier, one of the reasons more women don't become SheEOs is that we often have more fear around taking risks than men do. And that has to do with our interpretation of our abilities, which gets formed at a young age. How about you—how often do you find yourself avoiding challenges and playing it safe? What do you tell yourself—that you aren't smart enough? That you can't learn something?

It turns out that we also judge ourselves in a very different way than men do. According to research by Carole Dweck at Stanford University, bright fifth-grade girls, when given something to learn that was particularly challenging, were quick to give up—and the higher the girls' IQ, the *more* likely they were to throw in the towel. Bright boys, on the other hand, enjoyed the challenge of the difficult material and were more likely to work harder.

"Why does this happen?" writes Heidi Grant Halvorson, PhD, in her *Psychology Today* blog. "What makes smart girls more vulnerable, and less confident, when they should be the most confident kids in the room? At the fifth-grade level, girls routinely outperform boys in every subject, including math and science.... The only difference was how bright boys and girls *interpreted* difficulty....

"Researchers have uncovered the reason for this difference ... bright girls believe that their abilities are innate and unchangeable, while bright boys believe that they can develop ability through effort and practice."

Dweck speculates that these differences have to do with the differing ways boys and girls are raised. In her book *Mindset*, she describes these two ways of approaching learning as a fixed mindset (girls) and a growth mindset (boys). Her research shows that, regardless of gender, a fixed mindset often leads to plateauing early in life and never reaching one's full potential, while a growth mindset usually leads to increasing levels of performance and excellence.

Dweck has done extensive studies on how to cultivate a growth mindset regardless of your age or gender. Since her research is in education, she focuses on what parents and teachers can do to support a growth mindset in young people. These techniques apply equally well to entrepreneurs. Each of us can develop a growth mindset by adopting the following five attributes:

1. Believe that you can learn and focus on what you're learning in every situation.

2. Trust that your efforts to learn will pay off.

3. Persist despite setbacks.

4. See mistakes and feedback as learning opportunities.

5. Find inspiration from the success of others.

These practices are at the core of what I teach SheEOs, and what every SheEO who goes through our program comes out practicing on a daily basis. Depending on how you were raised, implementing these attitudes into your everyday life may be more or less challenging. If you find yourself doubting your efforts, deflating from feedback, feeling threatened by someone else's success, or wanting to collapse in the face of a failure, notice the thought and then remind yourself to see what's occurred as a positive lesson that will help you become even better. Over time, the more you do that, the more automatic this way of relating to the world will become.

PRACTICING GRATEFULNESS

Finally, as a way of integrating all of what you're learning as a SheEO, I'd like to suggest the practice of gratitude, which is something M.J. has written about in her book *Attitudes of Gratitude*. Gratitude is a totally free, unbelievably simple way to experience a sense of well-being and contentment on an ongoing basis. It takes no time or money, and it gives us a sense of uplift that helps generate energy to persist in whatever it is we're trying to create.

Research also shows that being grateful will help you integrate your self-care with ease. Folks who kept a weekly gratitude journal had fewer physical problems and exercised more regularly, ate better, and went for more regular checkups. It seems that when we recognize ourselves and our lives as the once-in-a-lifetime opportunity to make a difference in the world they truly are, we take better care of ourselves.

Gratitude is a powerful practice of noticing what's right, and even what's right about the difficulties we're experiencing. Like a growth mindset, it helps us mine everything as learning for ourselves. But it has another powerful effect. I've found that the more I'm grateful for the things that serve the purpose of what I'm trying to create and the outcomes I want, the more I get what I want. I start in the morning by asking, "What's my intention for the day?" Then in the evening, I look at everything that's happened that day with thankfulness, which closes the loop and keeps the mysterious mechanism working that brings me more of what I want and less of what I don't.

Respected mainstream researchers are proposing that reality is shaped by our minds. David L. Cooperrider, the Fairmount Minerals professor of social entrepreneurship at the Weatherhead School of Management, Case Western Reserve University, says that reality is "often profoundly created through our anticipatory images, values, plans, intentions, beliefs, and the like." In other words, we participate in creating what happens to us and our organizations through the power of our positive and negative imagery. Cooperrider's work on appreciative inquiry, in which you look at patterns of past success in order to create the future, is helping organizations around the world— from Green Mountain Coffee and World Vision to the U.S. Navy and Walmart—discover the power of appreciative and strength-based approaches to innovation and organizational design.

If you have employees, you can use the practice of appreciation to create better meetings and projects by simply asking, "What worked?" at the end of each so that you can track your patterns of success to use again. And over the long-term, by consistently applying this practice you can increase people's levels of engagement and performance and create greater profitability and productivity.

Based on ten million workplace interviews in 114 countries, the Gallup organization identified twelve questions whose answer in the affirmative correlated with workplace excellence. One of these questions has to do with strengths, as I talked about in Principle 4. Another is "In the last seven days have I received recognition or praise for doing good work?" Employees who answer no are twice as likely to quit in the next year. But there are bigger consequences for the organization beyond people leaving. Higher yes responses account for fewer mistakes and accidents, and a 10 to 20 percent difference in productivity and revenue. One large company calculated that each percentage point rise in the yes column for this question equated to hundreds of millions of dollars in sales. In fact, it's so powerful that Gallup identifies praise as the greatest lost opportunity in business today.

In a certain way, of course, the fact that praise affects the bottom line is obvious. If I tell you you're doing a good job, you'll feel motivated to keep on going and perhaps even work harder. But only recently has brain science confirmed why. When you receive praise or recognition, your brain releases dopamine, the chemical that gives you a sense of enjoyment and satisfaction. Brains crave dopamine, and people change their behavior unconsciously to get more. In a very real way, we're all working to get this "hit." That's why 44 percent of those surveyed find that compliments make them more productive. That's also why, in another large survey, 71 percent of workers said that praise was more important than money.

Making sure that you, and the folks who work with you and for you, get enough dopamine is important in other ways. It actually helps the brain make good decisions and choices. It's also crucial to memory and learning. When we don't get praised, success isn't leveraged or reinforced, and so our brain says, in effect, "There's nothing here, so let's move on."

Understanding this means that we need to rethink performance evaluations, which tend to focus on weaknesses. Gallup has found that praise supports strength-based development, which has been shown to create a 36.4 percent increase in performance over weakness-based approaches, which have a negative 26.8 percent impact on performance. That's a huge difference! So when someone you work with is doing something right—even if it's only once and not perfect—encourage them to continue to improve on that rather than focusing on what they've done wrong. Why? Because it helps to create a growth mindset, thereby increasing performance.

PRAISE HOW-TOS

- The effects of praise are short-lived, so it needs to be expressed frequently—daily at best, weekly at least.

- Aim for five expressions of positive feedback to every negative one. Research has shown that this ratio creates high-performing teams because it generates "grounded positivity."

- Praise must be specific to be effective. "Great job" doesn't work; the person won't necessarily know how it's great or what the results of his or her efforts were, and it can thereby reinforce a fixed mindset. So make sure that you include both the action and the effect. For instance: "When you stayed late to finish the report, it meant that our team could meet the deadline. I appreciate your persistence and hard work."

Two out of three women reported that they'd prefer to
have more free time than a bigger paycheck.
#IamASheEO

"Balance" creates the false belief in an achievable
equilibrium rather than recognizing our state
of flux. Integration.
#IamASheEO

You have your own business because
you want to live differently—so that you'll
have the flexibility to change the rules.
#IamASheEO

I'm differentiating myself as a SheEO by being an
advocate for integration. Recognizing the need to reflect.
#IamASheEO

It doesn't matter how you reflect, just that you do.
#IamASheEO

Self-care is not a dirty word.
#IamASheEO

What's your intention for the day?
#IamASheEO

Let's rethink performance evaluations, which are focused
on weakness, and support strength-based development.
#IamASheEO

PRINCIPLE

8
PRINCIPLE

IT'S A POST-HERO WORLD

We are all connected. To each other, biologically. To the earth, chemically. To the rest of the universe atomically.

—Neil deGrasse Tyson

Vanessa Reid is a co-creator of the Art of Participatory Leadership, a collaborative learning space in Greece that helps find creative answers to the country's complex problems. "There is just no way of going at this alone," she says. "I could never imagine 'leading' this. It's so complex ... none of us have the answers. Together we're more intelligent, and together we can create the conditions ... for the truly new to come through."

Like Vanessa, SheEOs know that we live in a post-hero world. In order to succeed not only in our individual endeavors but also in creating the kind of global transformation we need, we can't go it alone. We need other people to help us think boldly, to challenge our assumptions, to support us, to provide other unique perspectives, to offer guidance and experience. To get validation, to feel less alone. You can grow your business, yourself, and your impact much faster when you're getting help from others. Unfortunately, it's still true that women entrepreneurs have fewer mentors than men do. But we can level the playing field by using our natural tendency to turn toward other women for support.

Turning toward is a particularly female impulse, say researchers Laura Klein and Shelly Taylor. They've discovered that women respond to stress with brain chemicals that cause us to connect with other women. It's no wonder then that decades ago feminists created women's circles as a way to encourage one another to discover and enact their full potential.

The form of the circle itself represents an alternative to existing power models. In a circle, all members share power equally—a cooperative power structure that Jean Shinoda Bolen, a psychiatrist and circle activist, and others believe to be more natural to women than a hierarchical one. In the traditional male-dominated society, the dominant power paradigm is a triangle, a top-down structure in which a leader holds the most power. This way of being, Bolen argues, favors competition rather than cooperation. It also engenders a need to "save face," which has led to conflicts between people and between nations. Women's experience of power within circles is quite different, favoring equal access, communication, and connection. The experience of support within a circle changes the way women relate to one another and has a ripple effect into their communities and places of work. And such an experience, she contends, has the potential to change the way individuals relate to one another, share resources, and solve the global problems we face.

While feminists were at the forefront of the circle movement, both men and women are now coming to see that we have to move past the rugged individual hero model and work in groups. Ashoka, the largest network of social entrepreneurs in the world, is an interesting example of this transformation. Originally it supported only individuals—if you had two co-founders, for instance, you'd automatically be excluded. But then Ashoka's founder, Bill Drayton, and other senior leaders realized that they were only reinforcing an obsolete model. Now, as they say in their mission statement, they use a "team of teams" model to "address the fluidity of a rapidly evolving society." They believe that empathy and teamwork are among the critical skills needed to be successful in the modern world.

This doesn't mean you shouldn't be a solo entrepreneur but rather that if you're working alone most of the time, you need to find or create some kind of peer-to-peer network. That way you can maximize your chances of success and impact.

THE SheEO VISION

The need for connectedness is in part why I started SheEO—to mentor, guide, and support the next generation of women-led ventures on their own terms. I believe that the most powerful leaders are ones who know what they want, know what they're good at, and know who they need to surround themselves with in order to build a great team. Our programs have two main goals:

1. To develop confidence, boldness, and leadership ability of the next generation of women-led social ventures.

2. To connect young women entrepreneurs to a network of successful advisers and supporters who are committed to supporting their growth and the success of their businesses.

The SheEO program began as the SheEO Incubator, which was designed to help women bring clarity to what sort of impact they want to have in the world. As I've discussed earlier, we're also looking for new ways of financing that have a more feminine approach. So in the first SheEO cohort, we decided to bring together ten ventures funded by ten angels with philanthropic capital. Ten successful women invested $5000 each as a grant, creating a pool of $50,000 to be distributed to the cohort. It was our belief that it was important for the cohort themselves to determine how the money would be allocated. They were given only two parameters: you can't give all the money to one venture and you can't divide it up evenly among all the ventures.

Here's the process the first cohort followed, as described by one of the SheEOs:

> When we approached the SheEO fund allocation, we wanted to think about a collaborative model that would suit the culture and community we'd built over the course of the program. We wanted to ensure that we innovated a process that wouldn't be constrained by precedent models.
>
> **Step 1: Brainstorm**
>
> We sat in a circle as a group, openly discussing different ideas and brainstorming how we could allocate the $50,000. We discussed different scenarios and how we could allocate the funds in a way that we felt best supported us.

Step 2: Funding Criteria

We decided that we wanted the money to be used as efficiently as possible and cause an impact within the short-term, foreseeable future of six months. We also decided that we wanted every woman to receive funding, because as a result of the SheEO incubator program we developed a strong community in which we all felt supported. Our new model of doing business means that we work together and help everyone in the community be successful.

As a group we agreed that each SheEO would write up a clear list of the items she needed funding for in order to expand her business venture. Each SheEO would then pitch her request for funding to the rest of the cohort. There were three guidelines:

1. Each item must be put into action within six months of receiving the funds.

2. Each item must have visible, measurable results. Each SheEO needed to explain how each specific item would directly move her business venture forward.

3. The maximum amount of money each SheEO could request was $10,000.

Step 3: Group Forum

Everyone attended a group meeting in which each SheEO presented several different items that she requested funding for. Each SheEO had time to pitch and explain how funding would enhance her business venture. As a group we discussed every single item that was presented. There were many items that were questioned and altered. For example, when one person asked for resources to buy some video technology, someone in the group who had access to that technology offered to share rather than using precious resources to duplicate. Requests that didn't fit the criteria for funding were removed. The group discussed each request and openly shared feedback, concerns, and hesitations in allocating funds to it. If a request didn't fit the criteria, SheEOs offered advice, insights, professional connections, and resources for the most appropriate way to move each business venture forward.

We also tried to focus on the goods and services each of us needed rather than the market price of those goods or services. We tried to create opportunities for each of us to meet those needs outside the market realm, through pro bono or barter strategies. That way, the most important needs were all met, and the most important needs that could only be solved through funding were also met.

Step 4: Allocation of Funds

When all the SheEOs originally submitted their funding requests, the total amount of money being asked for was well over $50,000. After the group forum, the total amount was just under $50,000. This left a small sum of money, which we decided as a group to allocate evenly among all the business ventures.

When the cohort presented how they wanted to disperse the capital, they said they were really excited by what they had come up with. I asked them for the amounts per venture. They started to read out the numbers—$5086, $5386, $6436, and so on. I wrote them all down—and then I blew my top. "Really? What did we say was one of the parameters for dividing up the funding? 'Don't divide it up evenly....'. But $5086, $5386—isn't that pretty close to evenly? Is this you being bold? We just spent seven days working on your boldness and this is how you want to allocate funds?"

I still remember the looks on their faces. Some were upset that I was critiquing them. Others seemed ready to go back to the drawing board. They said they wanted to think about my feedback and that they needed some time. The other advisers and I left the room. We were called back later that day and told that they were standing by their decision. The cohort described the process they went through, which they hadn't done before, and explained that they felt this was the only way they could go. They felt that they were all amazing leaders, that they were all learning and creating an impact, and that they wanted to support one another to hit their goals. They also said, "We've decided to meet each month after the program ends and keep one another to our milestones. We also want to pay the venture money back so that more SheEOs can go through this program."

I was blown away. I thought to myself, "What group of guys in a room would have done this?" The model they'd come up with was about supporting one another and rising all tides, not just picking winners. Some ventures only got just over $1000 and some got almost $7000, but everyone was considered worthy and all were committed to keeping one another on track. As far as I was concerned, this was a huge success and the beginning of a new experiment.

Going forward, then, we'll do this with all our cohorts and see how the results change, or don't, over time. We need to keep experimenting—especially, as Red Burns says, in times of change. At SheEO, we're all about finding new methods and new approaches to redefine success in this new age of the creator, maker, and entrepreneur.

The SheEO program will continue to host cohorts for ventures that are early stage, have potential for scale, and require financing. As opposed to the traditional hierarchical organization, this is more of a biological model in which the cohorts are like pods in a networked organization. Each pod in turn creates its own mini-ecosystems— the one in India will have a different feel from the one in Toronto, for instance—and they're each part of a larger ecosystem.

This type of network—pods of ten all over the world, interconnected but distinct, learning the same principles but with their own special feel—is a model, I believe, for organizations in the future. That's why I wanted to create more pods than are possible using the angel investor paradigm and to offer support to many more women than just the small number who make it into a funded cohort. So SheEO will be launching workshops in schools, organizations, and corporations. And it will also offer cohorts that you can join online.

SheEO COHORTS

SheEO is a peer-to-peer network set up on a cohort model. A cohort is a group of people who share in a particular event during a particular time period. I like the notion of a cohort rather than a circle or a support group, because with a cohort you come in together at the same time, get bonded as a group, and go through something together.

My first experience with a cohort was when I was a kid. Every summer my parents would hire the same group of my brothers' and my friends, and together we'd do backbreaking farmwork. My parents were super smart to hire our friends, because we all commiserated together about this really brutal labour (planting hundreds of thousands of trees and weeding more than thirty acres of strawberries). Everyone who worked at the farm is bonded for life. We still get together, decades later, and we tell the same stories over and over and laugh and laugh. Being bonded in a shared experience is very powerful.

If you'd like to join a cohort, you can go to our website, www.IamaSheEO.com, to connect with other women in your region who want to form one. We provide materials to help you work through the principles and support one another in starting up your venture. Online tutorials, meetups, and other tools are also available to help you connect with one another and share what you're learning. At the end of the process, you'll be encouraged to present online and tape your pitch to share on the SheEO YouTube channel. This performance point is a crucial step.

I learned the importance of a performance point from Richard, who used to be a music teacher and has created hundreds of performances. He taught me that when you have a performance point, you rise to a higher level. I've seen how true that is in the entrepreneurial world. You can have all kinds of conversations in your group as you work through your meaning and values and business idea, but unless you actually have to present it, you don't rise to that next level of capability. And if you don't do a presentation, you don't get outside feedback to help you rise even more.

That's why it's really critical at the end of this process to put yourself onstage and present your business, as scary as it is. It's the beginning of having to show who you are, what you're doing, and how it's different and unique—which you'll need to do if you're going to find investors, partners, employees, and customers. Remember, as I said at the beginning of this journey, you have to live out loud. You can't hide under a rock if you want to be a SheEO. You have to demonstrate "why you, why now."

There are many ways to get support and advice in addition to being a part of a SheEO cohort. I'd like to highlight three. The first is creating a board of strategic advisers. The second is a partnership. The third is an entrepreneurial coach.

CIRCLE OF ADVISERS

A board of directors can help or hinder an entrepreneur, and many startup CEOs avoid them because they don't want their style cramped. But they can provide invaluable connections and expertise. I prefer a strategic circle of advisers who, unlike a board of directors, don't assume financial liabilities or require equity. Typically, they're experts who like to share their knowledge and don't expect compensation. Here are my suggestions for creating a circle of advisers worth having.

- Think about the gaps in your skills and look for people to fill those gaps. Each member should bring a different expertise.

- Choose people who've helped startups before. Those with a solely corporate background may not be able to offer help that's relevant.

- Make sure they've had advisory experience. Do they know what they're there to do? Will they offer strategic perspectives without trying to micromanage or demoralize you?

- Find out what kind of meetings work best for them. Do they want to come together once a month or quarter? Or would they prefer that you consult them individually? Would they rather have a conversation or receive an email? What kind of support do they want to offer? Making it work for them is important.

- Have a look at my mentor video here for some tips: www.youtube.com/watch?v=Of6UTxOPeBk.

PARTNERSHIPS

Having a partner in the business is another great way to not go it alone. Almost all the ventures I've created have been with partners. Typically we reach out to friends or family to partner with, which adds a level of complexity, to say the least. I've partnered with Richard in several endeavors, as well as my brother Matt and several friends. You'll know pretty quickly if partnering with family is for you. A lot of people have asked me how I could possibly partner with my husband, but it works so well for us. Based on my own experience, here are my thoughts on how to make it work—personally and professionally.

- Typically, partners come together because they're united in their vision of the business. But make sure you can agree on the smaller things as well—work styles, time commitments, roles and responsibilities.

- What will you do if you have a problem with the other person's performance? A commitment to work through any challenges honestly is crucial.

- Have a written partnership agreement that specifies what you're going to do if one of you wants to get out of the business. Life has a way of disrupting our best-laid plans, and if someday one of you needs to leave, owing to an illness, say, or a spouse's relocation, or a baby—or you decide you can no longer work together—it's much harder to decide how to end it in the heat of the moment than if you've agreed up front on the dissolution or sales process. I've known many entrepreneurs who end up paying dearly to end a partnership because they didn't have a written agreement. You can get inexpensive legal help and legal forms through companies like LegalZoom and Nolo.com. Make sure that any agreement you create covers the following five issues:

  1. *Capital Contribution:* How much money is each person putting in to start the business? What will happen if the business needs more money?

  2. *Salaries/Distributions:* When will the partners be able to take money out of the business? Will partners get repaid for their investment? If so, when?

  3. *Decision Making:* How will you make decisions, especially when you disagree?

  4. *Death/Disability:* Who would inherit your shares? Would they have a say in what happens to the company?

5. *Dissolution:* What happens if one of you wants to leave—
or the partnership isn't working for one person?

ENTREPRENEURIAL COACH

I'm a great believer in coaching. That's why I suggest that, as soon as you can afford it, you find yourself a great entrepreneurial coach. It's really hard to do this by yourself. A coach serves as a mirror, reflecting back things you may not be aware of. And if they're experienced, which they should be, they'll know the common pitfalls in the startup phase and help you avoid them. They provide a wider, outside perspective with no vested interest in your choices and decisions. Rather than bombard you with advice, they ask the kinds of questions that connect you to what you think and believe.

DEALING WITH ADVICE

While cohorts, networks, and advisers are incredibly useful, you need to approach the whole issue of advice carefully. I'm continually asking myself these two questions: "What conversations am I outgrowing? What kinds of conversations do I need to be having?" These questions help me get help that's truly useful rather than spinning my wheels hashing over the same perspectives. It's easy in a group to get stuck, especially in self-pity when something's not working, and to have other women in the group reinforce that. Part of how women often connect is by confirming one another's views of a situation: "Yes, that's terrible; yes, you're right...." To avoid that trap, I try to notice whether conversations are keeping me stuck. If so, it's a sign that I need to be talking to others who can help me move beyond my limiting point of view.

The other challenge we face in groups is getting bombarded by advice. I see this all the time with young women entrepreneurs in incubators and other mentorship groups. They get whiplash from one after another expert coming in and saying, "You should do this," "No, you should do that...." These young women start to do one thing and then totally pivot based on the next person to come along, till they lose all sense of what they should be doing. Rather than defining clearly what they want, they let everyone else define things.

I recently heard about a woman who was (unfortunately) a perfect example of taking bad advice. She had a business as a virtual assistant and was doing very well. But everyone around her said she should specialize in order to attract a particular type of client. So she tried it for a year until she almost went bankrupt. Then she went back to offering general services, and is finally getting back to her former success.

I once faced an advice-giving challenge in a program I was a mentor for. I was paired with another mentor who was exactly the opposite of me. I felt horrible for our team, because whatever the issue, we'd each have a totally different point of view on it. When I'd look at the team's faces it was clear they were thinking, "Help, just tell us what the right thing to do is, please!"

At first, I thought it was a terrible dynamic. But later I came to see that it was actually the fastest way for the mentees to identify what resonated with them. Because there was such a strong tension, they had to figure it out for themselves. I was talking to a very bright young man at one point, explaining how bad I felt about the team I was mentoring, and he said that upon reflection, the people he'd learned the most from were the people with a really strong point of view. It stopped me in my tracks because that was true for me, too. During the two years I was in a business relationship with a nightmare partner who had a very strong personality, I learned more about myself than in almost every other business relationship I've ever had. That partner pushed me to the limit in so many ways that I learned my boundaries and discovered who I was.

When considering advice, it's good to remember that no generalization is always true. No advice is necessarily right. I've seen many entrepreneurs hit it big and then never achieve success with another idea. It's partly luck, partly timing, partly the idea itself, and partly the combination of people all coming together. So rather than simply follow someone else's notion of what you should be doing, ultimately you have to do what seems right for you.

I've also seen this with brilliant young millennials. In many cases, overachievers are used to delivering exactly what's required to get the marks or be "successful," whatever that is. So when they're surrounded by advisers who've "done it before" or "been successful," they often tend to think these advisers know best. But I've seen people do exactly what their adviser tells them from the start, until one day they realize that it's basically the adviser running the company. And then they realize that they aren't really into it anymore because it isn't really their idea.

This can be particularly challenging for women because of our desire to please. If someone gives you an idea, you think you have to follow it. Many men have the opposite challenge—there's a huge number of young men doing startups who believe they need no help or advice at all. That creates a different set of problems.

I'm encouraging you to be aware of the female tendency to please and to take the mental time to question the advice you're being given. Instead of just blindly following, ask yourself, "Do I want to do that? Does it make sense to me in my context? Does it feel right? Is what I'm doing already working for me and giving me the results I want, while this idea is coming from the other person's notion of what I should be doing?" If the virtual assistant I talked about earlier had asked herself those questions before deciding to specialize, perhaps she would have ignored the advice.

Getting clear about whether what a person is saying is about them or you is also helpful. Remember the 90 Percent Rule: most of what someone suggests is about them. I had an adviser once who kept telling me that I needed more structure. What he was really saying was that if he were running my business, he'd need more structure. I operate best in a very fluid situation. So each time he'd say that, I'd think to myself, "Nope, that's not for me. There's my boundary again." It goes back to knowing who you are, how you best operate, and what you want—because all advice has to be evaluated through that lens.

Another way to evaluate whether something is for you is that when you do it, it doesn't feel right. Not awkward in the way that learning something new feels, but rather that it's fundamentally not right for you. For instance, there's all kind of advice out there on how to do pitches. I once hired someone to write a pitch slide deck for me, but when it came time to deliver the pitch to the VC, I did an absolutely terrible job. That's because when I read out the expert's words, they weren't mine. I didn't own it and therefore couldn't sell it. I'll never do that again!

If you're in a SheEO cohort, you can help one another notice when expert advice is getting you off track. That's partly why there are ten of you in a group—to help one another notice: "But I remember you saying you weren't passionate about that. I think you're doing it now just because that person told you to." "Oh, right. Okay. Thanks."

WHAT TO GET HELP WITH

Entrepreneurs, particularly at the early stages, tend to be jacks of all trades. You're the marketer, salesperson, graphic designer, web developer, and office manager. That's what you've got to do to make it, right? Wrong. Doing everything isn't the smart way to run your business. You just aren't going to be as good at certain things as others are, and so you'll waste time and get less stellar results than if you have an expert do it. It's also not smart for you to be doing nonessential tasks because they get in the way of rapid acceleration. It's focusing on doing what you're great at that will truly move the needle.

Why is doing everything yourself not a smart move? One economic reality that "thank-you-I'll-do-it-myself" entrepreneurs fail to consider is opportunity costs. These are the things you can't do, the opportunities you had to pass by, because you chose to do something else. Since they're invisible (how do you measure the funder you didn't find because you were at the copy shop?), it's easy to dismiss them. But you need to treat yourself as a precious, limited commodity that must be leveraged as strategically as possible. Your time and your mind are your biggest assets. Remember the energy-for-impact ratio. Keep just those things that are core to you and your business and that you need or want control over (and no, that doesn't mean everything!). The kinds of things you can avoid doing fall into three broad categories.

1. Things that require specialized knowledge you don't have, like legal, accounting, or technical knowledge.

2. Highly repetitive or mindless tasks, like data entry or running errands.

3. Tasks you don't enjoy or aren't good at. I generally don't believe in rules, but I do have a few. One of mine is "Don't spend five minutes doing something someone else could do in one." When I watch a person sit for an hour working on something that I know she could ask someone else to help her do in a few minutes, it makes me crazy. What a waste of brain power!

Can't afford help? This is also an engagement strategy. Meaning that, when you reach out to people who are really awesome at this particular thing, they'll now care about what you're doing and might even be able or want to contribute more. If you don't know folks who can help you, this is something your SheEO cohort might be willing to do for one another—create a "bank" of skills and talents that you trade when you need to: "I'll help you create a marketing strategy if you help me deal with my employee problem." Enlist your high schooler to create your PowerPoints or run errands. Or consider outsourcing. Given the global nature of the world we live in, you can find incredible expertise at amazingly affordable prices through a variety of outsourcing websites. Here are a few: Ask Sunday, Elance, VWorker (technical expertise), TaskRabbit, Virtual Assistant Board. That way you pay only for what you need when you need it.

CROWDTESTING

One other thing good SheEOs get help with is the viability of their idea or product through crowdtesting. Rather than spend a whole lot of your precious time, energy, and money only to discover that there isn't a market for what you've created, you go out and interview potential customers to see whether they'd buy it and for how much, what they like and dislike about your idea, and so on. Originally done by software and app developers, crowdtesting is now spreading to other entrepreneurs through the use of Twitter, Facebook, and other social media sites where you can throw an idea out there to get potential customer reaction. I love the idea because it aligns with my belief in not building something until there's a proven need. It's asking for help in a whole new way!

CELEBRATE YOUR GREATNESS

It's often hard to see our own gifts. One of the best ways a group can support one another is to have other people share what they see as your special qualities. That way, you come to own them more. At the end of your cohort, after everyone has presented, I suggest you create a SheEO plaque. Each person writes down three words describing each person's unique talents, gifts, and attributes. Then print it out, frame it, and put it on your desk or by your bed to remind you of just how special you are.

I'm sitting looking at mine now, and I'm always struck by how other people view me. It's important to own your greatness, and to be reminded of it during the tough times.

SheEOS' HOPES AND DREAMS

In the first SheEO cohort, Jane Roos created a gorgeous painting for the inaugural Honorary SheEO Award, which was presented to Ursula Burns, chairman and CEO of Xerox. Ursula is the first female African-American CEO of a Fortune 100 company. On the painting, the ten women in the program wrote their dreams for themselves as entrepreneurs. The ten women angels shared their own hopes and dreams for the next generation of SheEOs, and then Ursula shared her dreams. Here are their dreams:

Walk by faith, not by sight, focusing on ability, not disability.

To create healthy spaces.

To be the change the world needs.

I manifest my dreams into reality.

To see a world that values social impact as much as financial return.

To passionately drink life and still be unsated.

Define the next generation.

Real. Bold and free to be.

Peaceful and playful heart intelligence.

Eliminate obstacles for everyone to do good.

Leave behind more than you take away. Where you are is not who you are.

Never stop learning. Always be curious, do everything with passion.

To cultivate boldness, audacity, and humility.

Give more than you take.

Have the courage to be and live fully, way ahead, not closed.

To conceive, to believe, to achieve with others and for others.

To lead with courage, grace, and compassion for self and others.

I wish for all of us the wisdom to effect change and the courage to invest in trust.

To be true to yourself and others, to stand up for what you believe, to never give up.

To create a generation of leaders who support one another with integrity and confidence.

To lead with strength and grace in pursuit of excellence, creating spaces where wisdom and truth can surface to expand and unify the world.

What's your dream for you?

We can't go it alone—we need others to succeed
in our individual endeavors.
#IamASheEO

We have to move past the rugged individual hero model
and work in groups: the circle movement.
#IamASheEO

How can we reconcile advice? No generalization is
always true. No advice is necessarily right.
#IamASheEO

One economic reality that "thank-you-I'll-do-
it-myself" entrepreneurs fail to consider is the
opportunity costs of that role.
#IamASheEO

Own your greatness.
#IAmASheEO

What's your dream for you?
#IamASheEO

ACKNOWLEDGMENTS

To Patricia Karpas for being the catalyst, to M.J. Ryan for saying yes, to Anne-Marie Paquette, Mike Murchison, Tom Hadfield, Richard Ford, Matthew Saunders, Anne and Bill Saunders, and Abby for your honest feedback. To the countless number of wise elders who shared their insight along the way, including Dawna Markova, Cheri Huber, David Henry, John Rae-Grant, and Ortalia.

ABOUT THE AUTHOR

Vicki Saunders is the founder of SheEO. An entrepreneur, award-winning mentor, and adviser to the next generation of changemakers, she is a leading advocate for entrepreneurship as a way of creating positive transformation in the world. Vicki has co-founded four companies, including one that went public on the Toronto Stock Exchange. Vicki lives in Toronto with her husband, Richard Ford. You can find her online at **www.iamasheeo.com**.

www.iamasheeo.com